CONSTANTINE AMANTOS

PROLEGOMENA TO THE
HISTORY OF THE

BYZANTINE EMPIRE

Translated from the Second Greek Edition By
KENNETH JOHNSTONE

With a Preface By
CONSTANTINE TRYPANIS

ARGONAUT INC. PUBLISHERS
CHICAGO   MCMLXIX

Library of Congress Catalogue Card No. 67-17584

First Printing
January 1969

Manufactured in the United States of America

First American Edition

PREFACE

The reign of Constantine the Great (306-337 AD) has been rightly regarded as one of the major turning-points in history. For, by transferring the capital of the Roman Empire to Constantinople, Constantine succeeded in transplanting the Roman traditions of law and government to lands w h e r e language, literature and thought were all alike Greek; and, by accepting Christianity as the official religion of his empire, he built a state centered in a Christian capital and ruled by Christian kings, which was to last for a thousand years. Moreover, the move of the Roman capital to Byzantium was ultimately responsible for the later weakening of the empire by division, as a result of which the western half fell an easy prey to the Goths in 476 with far reaching consequences for Europe as a whole.

There is no doubt that the Byzantine Empire which emerged from Constantine's conception had its failings and its vices. It knew all too well palace revolts and the blinding and mutilation of opponents and it relished too intensively the festivities of the Hippodrome and interminable theological discussions. But its life was by no means a longdrawn death agony lasting over a thousand years, as the historians of older generations would have us believe. There were long periods of splendour and many unexpected revivals. In the sixth century, under Justinian, it turned once again the Mediterranean sea into a 'Roman Lake'; in the eighth, under the Isaurian dynasty, it checked the Eastern arm of Islam in its thrust towards Europe, thus saving the Western world for Christianity; in the tenth the stupendous victories of the Macedonian emperors over Saracen, Russian and Bulgar turned Byzantium into a great Eastern power, and in the twelfth Constantinople was once again a major centre of European politics.

Moreover, the great achievements in law, art and architecture of which Byzantium can boast are scarcely more remarkable than the influences it exercised upon the many peoples

who came into contact with it — Syrians, Copts, Armenians,
Georgians, Arabs, Bulgars, Russians, Roumanians, not to mention its fierce conquerors the Turks. Nor must the safeguard-
ing of the great treasures of classical Greek literature for
so many centuries be overlooked. By handing these over to
the scholars of the West and thus promoting the Renaissance,
Byzantium offered its last and perhaps its greatest service to
humanity.

For a real understanding not only of Byzantine history,
but of the history of civilization as a whole, the transition from
the ancient to the medieval Greek world is of paramount importance. It is this Amantos so skillfully traces in this *Introduction to Byzantine History*.

Constantine Amantos (1874-1960), sometimes professor of
Byzantine history at the University of Athens, Greece, undoubtedly remains the most distinguished of modern Greek
Byzantinists. Long years of research and teaching culmin-
ated in the publication of his *Byzantine History*, preceded by
his *Introduction to Byzantine History*, which is translated in the
present volume and is a quiet separate work. Both books
were favourably received by all specialists in the field, when
first published in Greek. Readers of this English version
will be quick to acknowledge the masterly assurance
with which the author leads us through the many
complex problems that underlay the great political, spiritual
and economic crisis of the late Roman world. In particular
they will observe with interest the influence of the East upon
the Greeks.

Greek history had been bound up with the East from its
very beginnings, from the Minoan and Mycenaean periods.
Admittedly, during the great centuries of the Greek spirit,
when under the leadership of Athens it achieved the highest
conception of freedom the world had known, Oriental influences retreated, but they made themselves felt with renewed
vigor after Alexander's conquests, when the Greeks penetrated
into the Orient they had conquered.

The cultured Alexandrian Greeks may have scorned the
ancient civilizations of Babylon and Egypt, yet despite themselves the powerful and subtle influence of the East permeat-
ed deeper and deeper the very fabric of their being, so that

their whole spiritual world became no more than a jungle of mystery-cults crowded with amulets, charms, adjurations and magic, which were vanquished only much later by Christianity, and even then not completely. Above all, in the south-eastern corner of the Mediterranean basin, in Egypt, Palestine and Syria, Greek nature became closely interwoven with that of the East, and here the seeds were sown, which were later to blossom in the new Greco-Oriental world of Byzantium.

So it came about that from the first century BC the Greeks gradually lost the clarity and independance of thought that had distinguished their classical age. This was to have a disastrous effect upon their Roman conquerors, who had looked to the Greeks for intellectual guidance. As soon as this failed, it was inevitable that the Roman world should have been brought to the desperate economic and political impasse of late antiquity. It was this situation that fostered the rise of Christianity. For the peoples, who had been so mercilessly exploited and humiliated by the Romans, turned to Christianity — religion of brotherly love and equality — for solace and guidance. In that general confusion and disenchantment the reign of Constantine the Great stands out like a milestone in history. So much did he do to alleviate the evils of his day.

All this as well as the far-reaching consequences of Constantine's reign are admirably treated in Amantos' *Introduction*. It is fortunate that this excellent book has found so able a translator as Mr. Kenneth Johnstone, whose knowledge of the Greek world is only outmatched by his admirable command of the English language. His translation will be an invaluable addition to the bibliography of Byzantine history, for which English-speaking readers will be especially grateful.

In conclusion, I should like to express the hope that it may not be long before the two volumes of Amantos' *Byzantine History* will be also translated into English.

C. A. TRYPANIS

Chicago 1968

CONTENTS

CHAPTER I

THE GREEKS BEFORE ALEXANDER THE GREAT

The Descent of the Greeks into Greece and their Dispersal

We cannot know in any detail the history of the descent of the Hellenes to the south from the Danubian lands. From excavations one can only just form some faint idea of the movements of peoples into the Greek lands during the prehistoric era. It seems certain that the older civilization of those lands, their wealth, their greater abundance of food and their milder climate attracted the Hellenes, who occupied with relative ease the southern portions of the Balkan peninsula. The Dorians, who alone among the Greeks had already acquired the use of iron, proved fatal to the older civilization of the region, but they imparted new life and creative force to the Greeks themselves. The descent towards the south was further accelerated by the pressure of new peoples coming from the north, the Illyrians and perhaps also, to some extent, the Thracians. Both Illyrians and Thracians mingled with the Greeks in the racial borderlands of Epirus and Macedonia, much as in later times an intermingling of Greeks and Albanians took place in the borderlands of Epirus and an intermingling of Greeks with Slavs and Bulgarians in the borderlands of Macedonia. This interfusion makes it hard to establish an exact ethnological definition of the Epirote and Macedonian tribes and has given rise to the vexed question of the origin of the Macedonians, the Paeonians and others.

The descent of the Greeks into the southern regions of what today is called the "Balkan" peninsula was of great historical significance. When the Greeks came to know the sea, they were fascinated by it, and using it as an easy means of communication, they spread abroad not only to the islands of the

1

Mediterranean from Cyprus to Sicily and throughout the Aegean and Ionian Seas, but also to the whole of the western Mediterranean coast, to southern Italy, and even to the Black Sea and to southern Gaul. That older trading nation, the Phoenician, was very easily evicted, since they had established no firm land bases but had conducted the purple-dyeing industry and the meagre commerce of those ancient times through the agency of a handful of settlers. It was only in the Semitic lands of Syria and Palestine and in Hamitic Egypt, as also in the western Mediterranean, where the Semitic Carthaginians were in control, that the Greeks were unable to expand. In Africa they occupied one region only, namely Cyrenaica, but they later founded small settlements in the islands of Dalmatia, which were not destined to flourish on account of the pressure of the uncivilized Illyrians.

This expansion of the Greeks aided their swift economic and intellectual development; later, through the agency of Alexander the Great, it carried them into Asia and took them further and further away from their ancient homeland, the northern Balkans.

From the time that the Greeks came to know the sea, and later Asia, they no longer felt the need to return to the north of the Balkan peninsula. Possibly, if Philip of Macedon had not died prematurely in 336 but had lived some years longer, he would have organized the Greeks of Europe more effectively and established them in the Balkans. Alexander, however, dispersed them into Asia and this dispersal exhausted the European Greeks who, even if they had not been subdued by the Romans, would have found it difficult to preserve their freedom from the Illyrians and the Gauls.

The Illyrians and Thracians

The expansion of the Greeks into Asia and the eastern Mediterranean hindered their closer association with the northern inhabitants of the Balkans, the Illyrians and Thracians, who were unable to derive much benefit from the proximity of the Greeks and remained uncivilized throughout. The few Greek cities among the Illyrians and Thracians — Stobi (Gradsko), Skopia (Skopje), the later Marcianopolis

(Devna near Varna), the Greek cities by the Black Sea —
were unable to exert any great influence on the country of
Illyrians and Thracians; nor could the rapid passage of
Alexander the Great through Thracian territory as far as
the Danube have any lasting civilizing effects. But it was
precisely because they were uncivilized, but were hardy
soldiers that the Roman power for centuries made use of
the Illyrians and Thracians for military service and by in-
tensive recruitment contributed to the thinning of the population.

Military recruitment and the lack of civilization aided the
decline of these peoples and later assisted the settlement
of the Slavs, who by degrees Slavized not only the Illyrians
and Thracians but also the Bulgarians who invaded the
peninsula later.

On account of its many difficulties and its excessive
conservatism the Greek language was unable to spread, and
except in a few cities it had no significant influence on the
Illyrians and Thracians. It is worth noting not only that
the Slavonic speech spread so easily among the Thracians
and Illyrians but that Latin too spread even as far as Dacia,
to the north of the Danube, where the Romans ruled from
the time of Trajan to that of Aurelian, that is to say no
more than a century and a half. The Latinized Illyrians and
Thracians, and the Aromouni or Roumanians, whom the
Slavs later also called Vlakhs, were subsequently hemmed
in by Slav expansion; but the numbers of them who have
survived in various parts of the Balkans up to the present
day show that the Latin tongue was easily imposed on the
Illyrians and Thracians, while in spite of the Byzantine domination Greek was unable to impose itself on the rural population but could only do so on the cities.

The descent of the Hellenes into Greece, then, carried
them on without difficulty into Asia and away from their
northern neighbours, the Illyrians and Thracians, who remained uncivilized, were thinned down by Roman recruitment,
and were Latinized and finally, to a large extent, Slavized.

Geographical Observations

Greece, their new home, exercised a great influence on
its new inhabitants, the Greeks. They quickly accepted the

ancient civilization of the country and the inhabitants mingled with the conquerors and formed a new racial blend. If
we take into account that men with fair hair and blue eyes
(for such the Hellenes coming from the north will have been,
in contrast to the dark-skinned older inhabitants) were rare
in ancient Greece, we must admit that the older elements
of the population, who had come to a large extent from Asia
Minor (Carians, Leleges, etc.), predominated in the mixture.
This diversity of elements in the population did not impede
the new development which was dictated by the geographical
structure of Greece. This is distinguished above all by its
variety; the alternation on a large scale of mountains with
plainlands and with countless bays and islands ensures an
inexhaustible variety of produce and a variety of life.

While in other countries, in Egypt for example, the mo-
notonous plain only affords a limited variety of produce and
a restricted manner of existence, in Greece it was easier to
develop the cultivation of a variety of products, as well as
navigation, trade and military and political life. While Egypt
made its inhabitants static, uniform (by tying them to the
given areas which fed them), Greece forced its inhabitants
to become mobile, receptive of new impressions, adaptable.[1]
Hence comes, too, a great resemblance between the ancient
and modern Greeks (both for better and for worse), in spite
of the frequent admixture of other races.[2]

The variety of the country and climate is typified by the
rich flora of Greece (perhaps the richest in Europe), which

[1] For the geographical influence of Greece, see: C. Neumann and J. Partsch,
*Physikalische Geographie von Griechenland mit besonderem Rücksicht auf
das Altertum*, Breslau, 1885, p. 9.; Otto Maull, *Griechisches Mittelmeergebiet*, 1922, p. 49; A. Philippson, *Das Mittelmeergebiet. Seine geographische
und kulturelle Eigenart*, 4th edn. 1922, p. 185; (see also A. Philippson,
"Griechenland und seine Stellung im Orient," *Geographische Zeitschrift*,
Vol. 3. Leipzig, 1897; V. Ehrenberg, "Griechisches Land und Griechischer
Staat," *Die Antike*, Vol. 3, 1927, p. 304 ff.; A. Zimmern, *The Greek Commonwealth. Politics and Economics in Fifth Century Athens*, 4th edn. Oxford,
p. 28 ff; Jardé, *La Formation du Peuple Grec*, 1923, p. 11; G. Glotz, *Histoire Grecque*, Vol. I, 1925 p. 2 ff.

[2] I append a few words more about the geographical structure of Greece.
First, geographical conditions can turn certain peoples into nomads, as for
example in Turkestan, Arabia, etc., or into sailors and traders, as in Greece.
The numerous islands and bays and the knowledge of the winds prevailing
in them made the Greeks into sailors very soon after they came down from

is not solely Mediterranean but in the more northerly mountainous regions is also a Central European and even an Alpine or mountain flora (from 6,000 ft. upwards). It is due to the varied geography of Greece that, according to Heldreich, there exists such a large number of purely Greek plants (Heldreich identifies over 600 of them, but still more are known to-day), which grow only in Greece, together with other European and Asiatic plants. The number of varieties of each plant is also very great, more particularly agricultural plants such as the vine, wheat, etc. Scientific agriculture is capable of developing specially selected qualities and, other considerations apart, has a great future before it in Greece.

Emigration

In ancient times, however, agriculture could not be developed in Greece, poverty was the constant companion of the Greeks and on this account settlers soon turned towards the routes opened to them by the sea. Even today many mountainous regions of the country suffer in a bad season,

the mountains. The inhabitants of Italy (and of Spain, France, etc.) with its few inlets and islands could not, and did not, easily become sailors and traders. The plains of Egypt and Roumania favoured serfdom and created the conditions of the fellahin, since they were engrossed by Pharaoh and the priests and great lords who used men as cattle in order to exploit the wealth of the soil. In Greece it was only in a few plainland regions, particularly in Thessaly and Messenia, that men were used as cattle by the "knightly" races of the Aleuades, Skopades, etc., and by the Spartiates. In the Greek mountains man remained free in his movements and this had beneficial results for the inhabitants of the country since they did not all become fellahin.

It is clear from the above that geographical conditions govern livelihood and the economic and political life of man. After the Greeks had thus easily become sailors and traders, they dispersed to the furthest ends of the Mediterranean, where they could live better than in their poverty-stricken mountains. But the geographical necessity which dispersed the Greeks brought them into contact with many other peoples, broadened their mental horizon and helped them to civilize themselves more rapidly and even to transmit their own civilization further afield with great rapidity.

The geographical parcellation of Greece prevented, too, the creation of any larger state and gave rise to a great number of small communities as well as to a great number of wars between them which, besides the considerable evils they entailed, brought with them one great blessing, the formation of political and moral character. These intestine conflicts provoked political conflicts and without them it would be hard to conceive the high degree of political and moral virtue reached in ancient Greece.

although by comparison with ancient times the disastrous effects of this are mitigated by trade and improved communications. Later, precautions were taken in the cities for the provision of corn at least, but in a time of dearth no one gave a thought to the mountain provinces. For this reason in particular, therefore, emigration became essential; political reasons, too, often enforced the willing or unwilling departure of colonists from Greece. The sea, which separated the islands from the mainland of Greece and from each other, as well as from western Asia Minor, served not as an obstacle but as an easy bridge for the movement of the Greeks. Without the Greek sea and its innumerable bays the Greeks could never have spread over the whole Orient and would never have become traders and sailors, but would have taken to the mountains and would have become mainly a pastoral people like the Illyrians and Thracians.

In the second millennium BC the Greeks contrived to spread not only to the islands of the Aegean but also to certain coastal districts of Asia Minor, particularly towards the south, to Pamphylia. In the first half of the first millennium BC, not only the whole of the western and northern shores of Asia Minor, Thrace, and the northern and western coasts of the Black Sea were occupied, but also Cyrenaica in Africa, part of Sicily and southern Italy, and southern Gaul. But it was the coastlands round the Aegean which were most easily opened up and constituted Hellas proper. This astounding maritime expansion and dispersal of the Greeks which, as we have said, permanently diverted the Greek world from the northern and central Balkans, delivered trade and navigation into their hands and ousted the Phoenicians, the Carians and the rest. The Black Sea colonies developed a prodigious trade, since they exported salted provisions, hides, slaves, corn and other wares to Greece in return for wine, oil, and other Greek agricultural or industrial products(textiles, pottery). This thriving trade made the Greeks indispensable to the barbarians who were themselves incapable of selling their own produce and of economic development. In many areas, as for example in the Aeolid of Asia Minor, the Greeks also developed agriculture (the same thing, in later times, happened in the city of Cydonia, where olive growing reached such a high state of development) but it was principally commerce and navigation which maintained the more distant Greek settlements. The incredible commercial expansion of Miletus is well known. The great trade which the Greeks developed through their colonies gave them a special character; it made them supremely a nation of business men, with all the individualism that implies. The much-travelled emigrant, who had many times risked his life and had come through, like another Odysseus, had a firmer individuality and could never be as docile as the Roman farmer or shepherd or the Slav herdsman. The emigrant, the sailor, the itinerant merchant developed far more quickly and easily than the static shepherd or farmer, and developed his fellow-citizens along with himself.

It was for this reason that both pre-Hellenic and Hellenic Greece developed so early from the intellectual and cultural point of view. But the overdevelopment of individualism [3] was a great obstacle to political organization and discipline, just as, on the contrary, Roman "majesty" was promoted by the blind docility of the individual. In no other country were so many political ideas so fully opened up for the first time, or so many political problems raised, although their solution and continuous application were made difficult and found themselves checked by the excessive freedom of the individual. Fortunately, there were still groups of farmers and herdsmen left in many parts of Greece, who kept the Greek world from the dissolution which befell the Phoenicians and the Carthaginians who were still more exclusively commercial than the Greeks. Mommsen,[4] wishing to explain the easy collapse of the Phoenicians, says that it was a consequence of their lack of instinct for political construction (Staatenbildender Trieb). I think, nevertheless, that if a people's way of life cultivates individualism and provokes the hostility of other peoples by exploiting them, this relaxes political discipline and finally causes the disintegration of the state.

The emigration of the Greeks had another great result, namely the diminution of their numbers. Those who went

---

[3] The various "Games" also encouraged personality and individuality. Plato's attempt to counteract individualism by means of his communistic ideas did not have a wide influence, just as the communistic system of Sparta (communal messes, limitation of private property, etc.) was not destined to prevail in Greece.

[4] Theodore Mommsen, *Römische Geschichte*, Vol. I, 10th edn., 1907, p. 587.

a long way away from Greece and never returned there
were mostly lost. To the colonies of South Russia, for example,
(Olbia, Chersonesus, and the rest) they undoubtedly took few
women with them, and consequently intermarried with the
local inhabitants. As a result the Greeks quickly became half-
Greek and half-barbarian — Graecosarmatians and Scythians.[5]
Only continual emigration from the mother-city reinforced
for centuries the Greek element in the distant colonies, which
would otherwise soon have lost their Greek character.

The Greek Colonies of the North

The Greeks of ancient South Russia were mostly settlers
from Miletus (except for the cities of Chersonesus and Phanagoria)[6] and were the first to conduct the trade between Scythia
and the Aegean. Through their settlements the Greeks became,
from the commercial point of view, the masters of the whole
of the Black Sea (Pontus), which came to be under the protection of Achilles, called for that reason "Lord of Pontus"
(Pontarches) and worshipped in the Greek settlements of
southern Russia. In the fourth century BC they also founded
in the Crimea the Greco-Scythian state of Bosporus, which
preserved its Greek character down to the fourth century AD.
The state of Bosporus, with its capital at Panticapaeum, held
the monopoly of corn, especially in the reign of King Leucon

---

[5] Herodotus (IV, 108) already knows of Greek half-castes: ". . . for the
Gelani (Geloni) were originally Greeks, but having removed from their
trading stations and settled among the Budini, they speak a language which
is partly Scythian and partly Greek."

[6] The oath of the Doric city of Chersonesus is famous (see also Minns,
Scythians and Greeks, p. 645). By it the Chersonesians bound themselves to
defend the freedom and democracy of the city and its dependencies, Kalos
Limen and the rest; not to betray any secret information (presumably
about military matters); to make provisions for food supplies, etc. The
people of Chersonesus swore "by Zeus, Earth, the Sun, the Virgin (i. e.
Athena), the Olympian gods and goddesses and the heroes who kept the
city, territory and walls of the Chersonesians" (i. e. the local heroes, Greeks
who had been granted heroic honours for great services rendered to the
city). It was a moving oath and shows the great solidarity of the remoter
Greeks which had its origin also in considerations of defence against their
barbarian neighbours.

Of the Greek · cities of southern Russia some had a democratic
constitution with a Boule, like Olbia and Chersonesus, others, like Panticapaeum, near the modern Kertch, developed for local reasons government
under a single competent man.

(389-349). It is needless to point out that the Greek cities of southern Russia had a great civilizing influence on the Scythians, a large number of whom they transformed from nomads into farmers.[7]

Later on, when corn began to be exported from Egypt to the Mediterranean and the Black Sea trade was restricted, the Greek cities of South Russia suffered great economic loss. But quite apart from their losses in the corn trade, the occasional raids of the Scythians helped towards the decline of the Greek cities, the chief among which were Olbia, Tyras, Chersonesus, Theodosia (the mediaeval Kaffa). Panticapaeum, Phanagoria, etc. This is clear from the *Borysthenitic Discourse* of Dio Chrysostom,[8] from which we likewise learn that even after these disasters fresh Greeks — those incorrigible emigrants — began all over again.

Settling by the river mouths, the Greeks took the whole fish and corn trade and the profits, it seems, were unlimited. They influenced the native inhabitants not only through commerce but because they served the requirements of the Scyth-

---

[7] Possibly, also, the cannibalism to which Strabo refers ceased on account of the civilizing influence of the Greek settlers. (Strabo, 298: ". . . for this sea (viz. the Black Sea) was then unnavigable and was called the 'Inhospitable' Sea (῎Αξεινος) owing to its storms and the savagery of·the peoples who lived round it, particularly the Scythians, who used to sacrifice strangers and eat human flesh and use skulls as drinking cups. Later, however, when the Ionians founded cities along the coast it was called the 'Hospitable' Sea (Εὔξεινος)." So it was the Greeks who changed the 'Inhospitable' into the 'Hospitable' Sea.

[8] See Arnim's edition, Vol. II (1896), p. 4: ". . . for being set as it is in the midst of the barbarians, (the city of the Borysthenites) is always at war and has often been taken, its last and greatest sack being not more than a hundred and fifty years ago." From the Acts of the Apostle Andrew (*Analecta Bollandiana*, 13,334) we learn certain information about the prime and the destruction of Theodosia: the Apostle Andrew "comes to a city called Theodosia which has a king called Sauromates. It was at that time populous with multitudes of Greeks and gloried in its philosophers, but now, given over to utter ruin, it is so desolated and destroyed that not a trace of humanity appears in it."

The Scythian nomads coming down from the steppes despised the cities and looked only for their destruction and looting. See the passage in *FHG* IV 196: "The Scythians used to mock at those who were shut up in cities on the ground that they did not lead a man's life but the life of birds perched up in their nests, and because they had deserted the land which fed them in favour of barren cities and had more confidence in lifeless walls than in themselves."

ians for manufactured goods. Scythians, for example, are represented as wearing their ornaments, their arms and so forth.

From the same work by Dio Chrysostom on Borosthenes (p.9) we learn the important fact that the Borysthenites, although they no longer spoke pure Greek, knew Homer's *Iliad* by heart and worshipped Homer "among other gods" and his hero Achilles as a god. Homer had not only made a god of his hero Achilles to these far-off Greeks, who had need of an ally in their struggles against the barbarians, but he had kept them tied to the Greek world.[9]

Further, it was not only along the whole Black Sea coast that the Greeks had settled for the exploitation of trade but on certain points on the Danube as well. Even at the modern Vintza, eastwards from Belgrade, Greek settlers were making use of the mineral deposits.[10]

Tartessus

Just as the services rendered by the Greek community to Russia did not prevent their annihilation, so a similar fate befell other distant Greek settlements. I would cite Tartessus, the Greek colony outside the Mediterranean beside the Spanish river Guadalquivir. Tartessus succeeded in founding a Greek state facing on the Atlantic Ocean, by exploiting the mineral resources of the Sierra Morena and the trade of the coastlands outside Gibraltar. We do not know the whole commercial and maritime history of the extraordinary Greek state of Tartessus, but it is clear, nevertheless, that it exercised a great civilizing influence on southern Spain.

Marseilles

Extraordinary, too, is the history of another remote Greek settlement, Massalia (Marseilles), which cornered the whole

[9] For the Greek communities in Russia see E. Minns, *Scythians and Greeks,* Cambridge 1913 and M. Rostovtseff, *Skythien und der Bosporus,* Vol. I. Berlin 1931.

[10] See V. Parvan, "La Pénétration Hellénique et Hellénistique dans la Vallée du Danube." *Bulletin de la Section Historique de l'Académie Roumaine,* Vol. X. (1923) p. 1.; *Revue Internationale des Études Balkaniques,* Vol. I. p. 65.

trade of southern Gaul and founded a number of cities in that area which have survived to this day: Agathe (now Agde), Olbia (Eoube), Antipolis (Antibes), Nicaea, (Nice), the Stoi-chades (Lérins) Islands, Tauroentium (Taurents), etc.

Nicaea was founded in commemoration of a victory over the Ligurians. In spite of its many enemies, the Carthaginians (the Massaliotes fought the Carthaginians and Etruscans off Alalia in Corsica in 540 and won a "Cadmean victory," according to Herodotus (I. 166)), the Ligurians and the Tyrrhenians or Etruscans from Italy, Massalia was able to keep its position of commercial supremacy in the western Mediterranean. In addition to its settlements in Gaul it also sent small colonies to Spain, and profited greatly from the trade in minerals. Its trading vessels even emerged onto the Atlantic coasts in pur-suit of the famous discoveries made by its great seamen Euthy-menes and Pytheas.[11] The cultural influence of Massalia and the economic development of southern Gaul made the Greeks acceptable there. According to Strabo (181) " . . . all the educated classes (i. e. among the Massaliotes) are given to the art of speaking and to philosophy, so that, whereas a little time ago the city was merely given up to being a school for the barbarians and indeed made the Gauls so favourable to Greek ways that they actually wrote their contracts in Greek, nowadays it has induced the foremost of the Romans who are interested in learning to go there to study instead of going to stay at Athens." [12]

[11] Pytheas sailed round Great Britian, reached Thule (Ireland) and even entered the Baltic. See G. Broche, *Pythéas le Massaliote, Découvreur de l' Extréme Occident et du Nord de l'Europe au IV. Siécle avant J. Christ*, Paris 1936.

[12] Attention may also be drawn to the following beautiful epitaph from Gaul, as a memorial to the Greek community there (*Inscriptiones Graecae Siciliae et Italiae*, ed. Kaibel No. 2508):

> ἄνθεα πολλὰ γένοιτο νεοδμήτῳ ἐπὶ τύμβῳ·
> μὴ βάτος αἰχμηρὴ, μὴ κακὸν αἰγίπυρον,
> ἀλλ' ἴα καὶ σάμψουχα καὶ ὑδατίνη νάρκισσος,
> Οὐείβιε, καὶ περὶ σοῦ πάντα γένοιτο ρόδα

(May there be many flowers on this new-built tomb, not rough bramble nor that weed the rest-harrow, but violets and marjoram and the water-loving narcissus, and all about you, Vaebius, may there be roses.)
Rough brambles chocked the Greek community in Gaul, as they did every-where else where this community was intermingled with many foreign elements.

The representative system of government is also interesting. According to Strabo (179) the Massaliotes " . . . are
the best governed of all," by a "Council" or Parliament of six
hundred men called τιμοῦχοι , from whom the Government
are elected. The τιμοῦχοι had to be fathers of families and
must have been citizens for three generations (διὰ τριγονίας).
The Councillors of the Massaliotes were not lightly replaced:
consequently there were continuity and experience in the
city's policy and to this, beyond doubt, its great cultural
achievements were due. The independence and the civilizing
work of Massalia were destroyed by the conqueror of Gaul,
Julius Caesar

Magna Graecia

In this short survey of the Greek settlements we can, of
necessity, refer only to the peripheral points of the Greek
dispersal. We cannot enlarge on the history of the Greeks of
Sicily and Italy, which is in any case better known. It must
be enough to indicate that the Greeks of Italy found a more
fertile country and developed an intense economic life.
They founded famous cities (Syracuse, Akragas, Tarentum,
Croton, and others); they built magnificent temples. The
wealth of these Greeks also appears on their coinage, on
which an ear of corn and other products of the country figure frequently. The prosperity of the Greek community allowed them to keep pace with the civilization of Greece proper, [13] to summon philosophers and poets from Greece to instruct them, and themselves to contribute from their own intellectual resources to the fulfillment of the Greek mission.
It was through the Greeks of Italy that civilization was first
and by degrees transmitted to the Romans, who thus became
capable at a later date of reducing their benefactors to sub-

13 The earlier Greek emigrants to Italy intermingled, of course, with the
people of the country and became half-caste Greeks, but without forgetting
their Greek origin. A moving incident is referred to by Athenaeus (XIV.
632a): "It has so happened that the Posidonians, who live on the Tyrrhenian Gulf and who were originally Greeks, have been completely barbarized
and have become Tyrrhenians or Romans. They have even changed their
language and all but one of their customs. But they still keep one Greek
festival even today when they meet to recall those old names and customs
of theirs, and having lamented and wept over them to each other, they
depart."

mission. But of Greek influence on the Romans more will be said later.

Egypt and Cyrenaica

The Greeks were unable to expand freely in Africa mainly on account of the resistance of the Semites (Carthaginians), and at an earlier stage on account of the Egyptians also. From the sixth century BC Egypt too permitted settlement and trade and the Milesians were the first to found a Greek settlement with the characteristic name of Naucratis (Sea Power). Psammetichus even had Greek mercenaries, while Amasis took a Greek wife from Cyrene. Later, the trade attracted other Greeks as well, who did not found other settlements of their own but merely established a single common centre and temple, the Hellenion, where they gathered for their festivals and settled their disputes through arbiters. The Hellenion was a reminder to the Greeks of their common origin and their common homeland and united them in this foreign country.

To the west of Egypt the Greeks, particularly the Dorians, founded settlements on the Cyrenaic peninsula and exploited the medicinal and aromatic plant called silphium and the other products of the country. In 155 BC the king of Cyrene, the younger Ptolemy, who was at the time the ruler of Egypt also, as Ptolemy the Stout (Physkon), drew up a will by which he left his dominions to the Romans in the event of his leaving no heirs: "Should any of the accidents of mortality befall me before I leave successors to my kingdom, I leave the kingdom which pertains to me to the Romans, with whom I have kept friendship and alliance in all sincerity from the beginning." The Greek community in Cyrene was preserved until the beginning of the fifth century AD. The famous bishop and scholar Synesius was its last defender against the incursions and attacks of the native Africans.

CHAPTER II

THE GREEKS AFTER ALEXANDER THE GREAT

Philip and Alexander

Up to the end of the fourth century BC the Greeks spread out along the shores of the Mediterranean and the Black Sea and exercise a virtual monopoly of the commerce of those seas. From the time of Alexander the Great onward, Asia and Egypt pass under the political control of the Greeks and the world situation shifts, much as it did after the discovery of America and its exploitation by Europe. But the exploitation of Asia by the Greeks brought about the exhaustion of the European Greeks, their subjugation to the Romans and their surrender to Asian influences.

The assassination of Philip (336 BC) was a great disaster for the Greek world. Few gave him his due while he lived and the brilliance of his son was to overshadow him after his death. A later age has with difficulty come to appreciate the true worth of that deep thinker Isocrates whose aim was to put an end to the war fever of the Greeks (*Philip*, 88), to unite the Greek world through Philip's agency and to seize and colonize western Asia Minor.[14] Besides Isocrates, men like Phocion, Aeschines, the historian Theopompus, and later Polybius (IX, 33) appreciated Philip's true worth. If Philip had lived longer, not only would his great achievement, the unification of the Greek world, have been firmly established, but Greek expansion would have attained its natural frontier in the Balkan Peninsula, where he had already founded set-

[14] Nevertheless, after the battle of Chaeronea (338 BC) and the threat of a Macedonian invasion of vanquished Athens, Isocrates, then over 97 years of age, refused to eat and died within a few days. He had sought the unification of the Greeks through Philip, but he had no desire to see Athens humiliated and despoiled.

tlements, Philippopolis (Plovdiv) and others.

Philip's wars against the Illyrians afford a typical illustration of this. In 359 Philip's brother, Perdiccas, fell in battle against them in the plain of Pelagonia. In 357 Philip himself, with the general Parmenion, overcame the king of the Illyrians, Bardylis, in the plain of Florina. In 352 he won a victory over another Illyrian king, Cleitus, and founded Heraclea, not far from the modern Florina. In 344 he again waged war on the Illyrians under the command of Pleuratus, and on this occasion Alexander overcome them. Had it not been for Philip and Alexander, the Illyrians would in all probability have occupied Macedonia and the course of Greek history would have been different.[15]

After Philip's death the control of the Greek world was taken over by Alexander, who was, as Eduard Meyer has said, a blend of two heroes — Achilles and Hercules; by him Greek influence was projected as far as India and Turkestan, a dissipation which led to the tragic exhaustion of the Macedonians and the other European Greeks.

It is certainly open to question whether Philip would have made a mere promenade as far as the Danube, as Alexander the Great did.[16] It seems more likely that he would have insisted more strongly on the reinforcing of the Greek element in the Balkans and would not have directed his gaze so romantically towards the occupation of Persia and the taking of vengeance on that country.

The relation between Greeks and Persians before Alexander the Great had not been exclusively hostile. Many Greeks had served the Persian Empire and many had lived freely there. About the end of the sixth century (508), the geographer Scylax of Caryanda had studied the coastline of the Persian Empire on the Indian Ocean and had helped to bring Indian peoples into submission to the Persians. The Rhodian brothers, the generals Mentor and Memnon, and some thousands of Greek soldiers had served the Persians and even defended them against the attacks of Alexander. Physicians like Ctesias

[15] On Philip, see A. Keramopoulos, *A Short History of Philip the Second of Macedon* (in Greek), Athens 1935; V. Chapot, "Philippe II," in *Hommes d'Etat* by A. Diff and F. Galy, 1936.

[16] See N. Vulci, "Alexandre le Grand sur le Danube" in *Xenia of the University of Athens*, p. 181.

served in Persia; and among other things, Persian religious ideas had entered Asia Minor and had been accepted by the Greeks there. In fact, despite all the enmity between Persians and Greeks, these two Indo-Germanic peoples had contrived to draw closer together even before Alexander's time.[17]

The ease with which Alexander the Great dissolved the complex racial amalgam of the Persian Empire is significant; significant too is the ease with which he drew together not only Greeks and Persians but other peoples as well. The cosmopolitan government of Alexander's vast empire, as contrasted with the racial fanaticism which had marked the beginning of his expedition, derived from his need to make use of Asiatic soldiers, since he could not go on bringing hoplites over from Macedonia. But Alexander's power was further strengthened by the utilization of the enormous hidden treasures of the Persian kings, the milliards of drachmae which he put into circulation and which immediately fortified the economic life and trade of Asia.

Alexander's whirlwind conquest and his founding of cities, the influence of Greek art and the whole of Alexander's great work of civilization in general made him a legendary hero to the peoples of Asia. Centuries after Alexander, there was written, under the name of Callisthenes, nephew of Aristotle, a history *romancée*, describing in an imaginative fashion the wars and achievements of the great Macedonian. This Pseudo-Callisthenes succeeded in publicizing and popularizing the name of Alexander the Great, which passed into Arabic and Persian poetry and into the traditions and legends of a variety of peoples. Even to-day, in certain regions of Afghanistan, Greek gold coins of the time of Alexander are

---

[17] See L. Stella. "Eraclito, Efeco e l'Oriente," *Rendiconti della R. Accademia dei Lincei*, 1922, p. 521. In this interesting article the probable assertion is made that Heraclitus came under the influence of Zoroastrianism in Asia Minor and as a result propounded his "War (strife) is the father of all things." It was this doctrine too which caused him always to expect the greatest benefits from the clash of opposites. It is true enough that the Zoroastrian conception of conflict could not have failed to please the Greeks and if only Xerxes and his generals had never extended their power as far as Greece and thus created an unbridgeable chasm of racial hatred, we can take it as highly probable than the dualistic conceptions of Zoroastrianism would rapidly have spread to Greece.

in circulation and legends are current concerning him.[18]

The Founding of Cities

It is no less significant that Alexander founded cities and planted Greek soldiers not only in Asia Minor but far away in Egypt and above all in Persia and further east.[19] By promoting security the founding of cities was also of advantage to trade; further, according to the ancient Greek conception it was indispensable to the diffusion of civilization as well as to the rapprochement and intermingling of peoples (especially the Persians and the Greeks). Cities founded by Alexander have survived to our own day, Herat, for example (Alexandria Arion), Merv (Alexandria Margiane), Alexandria Arachoton (Kandahar), Alexandria Sogdiane (Khodjend), and others. Thirty cities were founded with the name of Alexandria.

Naturally not all of the cities founded in Asia had the artistic wealth of the great capitals; nevertheless they were adorned with gymnasia, baths, temples and theatres and afforded the greatest possible contrast to the countryside. In this connection we may take note of part of a description of the metropolitan city of Smyrna, as an indication of its magnificence. Aelius writes (XV); "... for the whole place right down to the seashore is bright with gymnasia, market squares, theatres, gardens, harbours, and with natural and artificial beauties vying with each other ... there are so many baths that you might well be at a loss which one to bathe in ... there are springs and fountains ... and an inexpressible abundance of theatres of all kinds, both for plays and for other spectacles."

The system of urbanization, which was also followed by

[18] See A. A. Pallis. *The Book of Alexander the Great* (in Greek), Athens 1935 (with a number of illustrations on the subject). Bissing, *Das Griechentum und seine Weltmission,* 1921, p. 50.

[19] According to Polybius (X. 27.3): "Media . . . is surrounded by a belt of Greek cities founded by Alexander's bodyguard to protect it against the barbarians who neighbour it." And according to Diodorus Siculus (XVIII.4, 4) Alexander made "groupings of cities and transfers of populations from Asia to Europe, and conversely from Europe to Asia, in order to bring the largest of the continents into a common harmony and kinsmanly friendship by intermarriage and by intimate association."

the successors of Alexander (the Diadochi), attracted the Greeks to Asia by its administrative independence, its security and its economic advantages and a lively movement began of Greeks emigrating from Europe to Asia similar to the emigration of Europeans to America in the nineteenth century. It was the first time that so many cities had been founded in Asia, since, apart from Babylon, Nineveh and a few smaller towns, the population of Asia and even of Mesopotamia had previously dwelt in village communities.[20]

The Greeks in Turkestan and India

The final conquests of Alexander in the direction of the modern Turkestan and India were destined to form remarkable Greco-barbarian states. About 255 BC the governor of Bactria, Diodotus, separated from the Seleucid Kingdom and founded a state of his own: as an independent monarch, he received the additional name Soter (Saviour), perhaps on account of his success in conflict with the nomads of Asia. We have only an imperfect knowledge of the history of the kings of Bactria, our most authoritative source being the fine coinage which bears witness that good Greek artists were summoned to the extreme limits of the Greek dominion in Asia. The founding of an empire by the Parthians, who were nomad kinsmen of the Persians (249 BC), under the Arsacid dynasty separated the Greek kingdom of Bactria from the Seleucids and doomed it to a speedier death. We know from coins about thirty names of Greek kings of Bactria, by whom new cities were founded.[21] But the work of Greek civilization in Bactria came to nothing. The kingdom was

[20] Pliny. *Nat. Hist.* VI. 117: "The whole of Mesopotamia used to belong to the Assyrians and the population was distributed in scattered villages, except for Babylon and Nineveh. The Macedonians gathered the population into cities on account of the fertility of the soil." See too V. Tscherikower, *Die Hellenistische Städtegründung von Alexander dem Grossen bis auf die Römerzeit.* 1927. A. Jones, *The Cities of the Eastern Roman Provinces.* Oxford, 1937. See also L. Robert, *Villes d'Asie Mineure.* Paris. 1935.

[21] Louis de la Vallée-Poussin, *L'Inde aux temps de Mauryas et des Barbares Grecs, Scythes, Parthes et Yue-Tchi.* 1930, pp. 230 and 241. P. Gardner *The Coins of the Greek and Scythic Kings of Bactria and India* 1886 (Repr. 1966). W. Tarn, *The Greeks in Bactria and India,* Cambridge 1938. The last book of Prof Tarn shed further light on the outposts of the Greek world and their great personalities.

subdued by the nomad Tokhars about 128 BC, and only the Indian extension of the Greek Empire lasted on a while longer, until 50 BC. Bilingual coins were struck in India, in Greek and in Indian, on which the kings are commonly given the title of Soter. We shall see later the great influence exerted by Greek artists on the development of Buddhist religious art. But all the Greek cultural activity in India could not avail to save the far-flung Greek sphere of influence there, which was subjugated by the "Indoscythians" after some three centuries of struggle. Thus, step by step, unlamented and friendless, all those distant Greek communities were lost, which Alexander's eagle flight had torn away and carried so far from the bosom of their mother Greece.

The Settlements of the Diadochi

The successors of Alexander did not all follow the same policy. They did not all found cities, nor did they all pursue a similar policy of drawing their peoples closer together. It was the Seleucids who followed most faithfully the policy of Alexander the Great; it was they, too, who founded the greatest of the Greek states, extending from the Hellespont to India. They made racial rapprochement their aim and founded a vast number of settlements on a systematic plan. Seleucus and Antiochus were the greatest founders of cities in history.[22] The intermingling of the Greeks and the Syrians had extremely fruitful cultural consequences, since it was from Syria that most of the leading cultural figures came in the second and later centuries[23] and it was from Syria, later, that Arabic civilization was derived. According to Appian (*Roman History: Syria*) the oracle of Appollo of Didyma in Asia Minor advised Seleucus not to seek to cross into

[22] Eduard Meyer. *Blüte und Niedergang des Hellenismus in Asien*, 1925. p. 20.

[23] R. von Scala "Das Griechentum seit Alexander dem Grossen." Helmolt-Tille, *Weltgeschichte*. Vol. IV. 1920. p. 105) judges the case more severely: "The Greco-Syrian conception of the "single nature" spread throughout Syria, which devoted itself to the pursuit of wealth and gave itself over to pleasure and to degenerate forms of art. It was perhaps for this reason that Christianity came to birth in this region as a deliverance from an intolerable way of life."

Europe since Asia was better and was sufficient for him. (Μὴ σπεῦδ' Εὐρώπην δ', 'Ασία τοι πολλὸν ἄμεινον).

Thenceforward he began to found cities which he named after the members of his family or after leading cities of old Macedonia. Thus, according to Appian, Seleucus founded sixteen Antiochs in honor of his father Antiochus (of which the Antioch on the Orontes river later became a huge city of the utmost importance), five Laodiceas in honour of his mother Laodice, Apameas in honour of his wife, and Seleucia on the Tigris in his own name, which ousted ancient Babylon as capital and likewise became a huge city. Other cities received Macedonian names: Berrhoea (Aleppo), Edessa, Pella, Amphipolis, Europus, Cyrrhus, Arethusa; and two cities took from victories of Seleucus the names of Nicephorion and Nicopolis.[24] The country along the Orontes was called Pieria.

The Seleucids founded many cities in Asia Minor which were more of the nature of military settlements. Seleucus was the original founder of Magnesia below Mount Sipylus and of Thyateira, Antiochus of Apamea on the Maeander, Laodicea, Stratonicea and Antioch. After the Seleucids the Attalids (from 283 BC) founded Attalia and a number of other cities in Asia Minor and the example set by these Greek rulers was followed by semi-barbarian rulers as well. Thus, the ruler of Bithynia, Nicomedes, founded Nicomedia in 264 BC and the rulers of Pontus and Cappadocia similarly reinforced Greek cultural influence and imitated and spread Greek civilization.[25] The ruler of Armenia, Arsames, founded in the Greek manner Arsamosata on the Euphrates (240 BC), while Tigranes

---

[24] Appian (*Syria* 57): "(Seleucus) founded cities throughout the whole length of his empire — 16 Antiochs in honour of his father; five Laodiceas in honour of his mother; nine in his own name; and four in the names of his wives, three Apameas and one Stratonicea. The most celebrated of them today are the Seleucia on the seacoast and the one on the river Tigris, the Laodicea in Phoenicia, the Antioch under Mount Lebanon and the Syrian Apamea. The rest he called after Greek or Macedonian cities or after achievements of his own or in honour of Alexander the King. Hence it comes that there are many Greek and Macedonian city names in Syria and in the barbarian lands beyond it: Berrhoea, Edessa, Perinthus, Maronea, Kallipolis, Achaea, Pella, Oropus (Europus), Amphipolis, Arethusa, Astacus, Tegea, Chalcis, Larissa, Heraea, Apollonia, and among the Scythians Alexandreschata; and in honour of Seleucus's own victories there are Nicephorion in Mesopotamia and Nicopolis in the part of Armenia nearest Cappadocia."

later removed the population of Mazaki (then the Cappadocian
Caesarea) and other cities to Tigranocerta (then called Mar-
tyropolis), according to Strabo, (539) who tells us that the
Mazacenes used the laws of Harondas.[26] They thus became
still more Hellenized.

The Hellenization of Asia Minor

The numerous Greek settlements which were founded on
the main centers of communication in Asia Minor(ubi via,
ibi colonia, according to Radet) and in the fertile regions
radically altered the life of the country. After the founding of
so many cities, a large nomadic population could be settled
near them and stabilized, since they found work in the
cities and sold their produce. But the accumulation of nomads
near the cities, and even in them, as well as the descent of
the villagers from their poverty-stricken villages greatly helped the Hellenization of the country. The people of Asia Minor
had not the same spirit of resistance to Hellenism which was
shown by the Jews and the Egyptians; they yielded easily
and were assimilated. Additional factors which contributed to
this were certainly the ancient cities of the coast, which had
almost come to surround Asia Minor, and the kinship of
certain peoples (the Phrygians, for example) which made
rapprochement and assimilation easier.   The older Carians,
Lydians and Mysians had been practically Hellenized before
Alexander's time. For all these reasons, and above all on account of the founding of so many cities, Asia Minor was the
only country which the Greeks managed to Hellenize to such
an extent as to make of it later the backbone of the Byzantine
Empire for nearly a thousand years. But here, too, the work

25 According to Diodorus Siculus (XXXI. 19.8) Ariarathes VI, the ruler of
Cappadocia "besides displaying a most praiseworthy conduct of life in other
ways, also became an adherent of philosophy, and under him Cappadocia,
which was quite unknown among the Greeks, became a home even to the
educated."

26 Strabo, 539: "The Mazacenes use the laws of Harondas and also appoint
a Reader in Law who is an interpreter of the laws among them, like the
Jurisconsults among the Romans. But Tigranes the Armenian treated them
shabbily when he overran Cappadocia: he transferred them all to Mesopotamia and formed the grater part of the population of Tigranocerta out of
them. Those who could return home later on, after the capture of Tigranocerta.

of Hellenization was not achieved with the same speed and
uniformity everywhere. The favour shown by the Romans to
the Greek population, Christianity [27] and the Byzantine Empire beside were needed to bring the process of Hellenization
to completion. In Pontus it was completed in the thirteenth
century in the Empire of Trebizond; in Cappadocia the Greek
dialect which survived with an admixture of barbarisms shows
the incompleteness of the linguistic assimilation.

Syria

Nevertheless, despite the slowness and the incompleteness
of the Hellenizing process, we repeat that no other country
was Hellenized to the same extent as Asia Minor. The case
was otherwise in Syria and Mesopotamia (although some hundred cities were founded in northern Syria). Greek was spoken
there only in the cities, while the villagers, shepherds, farmers and the like spoke the Syrian or Aramaic language. Syrians,
Jews or Babylonians were only Hellenized in so far as they
took to city life and acquired even a smattering of letters.
Where the country population was numerous, Aramaic gradually came to be spoken in the towns, whose resident merchants needed to attract customers from the countryside, by
the use of Aramaic among other things. For this reason Greek
culture did not make in Syria or Mesopotamia the progress it
made in Asia Minor. In these provinces only the upper classes
in the towns came under Greek influence. In consequence,
when the Arabs arrived later, Greek was rapidly forgotten, and
many Greeks adopted the Arabic tongue, as the Syrians did.

In spite of the incredible and historically unique civilizing influence which the Greeks exercised in Asia, that influence was destined rapidly to lose its holding power under pressure from three adversaries — the Romans, the Parthians and
the Semites (Nabataeans and Syrians).

Antiochus III, the Great (223-187 BC) was the man most
fitted to continue the work of Alexander the Great and to
preserve the unity of the Greeks in Asia. He occupied

---

[27] The Isaurians, the Lycaonians and other native peoples of Asia Minor
continued to speak their own Asiatic language for many centuries after
Christ. See K. Hall. "Das Fortleben der Volksprachen in Kleinasien in
nachchristlicher Zeit." *Hermes.* Vol. 43. (1908) p. 240.

the whole of Asia Minor, overcame the Parthians (208) and took possession of Phoenicia and Palestine. The Romans alone defeated Antiochus, at Magnesia in Asia Minor (190 BC): they thus strengthened the resistance of the native peoples and halted the expansion of Greek influence in spite of all the ability shown by the Seleucids.

Antiochus IV Epiphanes (175 - 163 BC) was educated at Athens and returned to Asia more Greek than ever. He lived not as an Asian king but as a democratic Greek citizen and wished to impose Greek customs, Greek religion and the Greek language. He even Hellenized the local gods. In Jerusalem he enforced the worship of Olympian Zeus in place of Jehovah, though under the protection of a Greek guard. The Jews began a desperate struggle against Hellenization, a struggle which was subsequently taken up by other Semitic peoples also, the Nabataeans and the Syrians themselves under the governors of Edessa, between the Tigris and the Euphrates.

Antiochus VII Sidetes (138 - 129 BC) captured Jerusalem and defeated the Parthians, but was taken by surprise through his own negligence and was defeated in spite of his heroic resistance. Phraates, the vanquisher of Antiochus, wished to use his Greek prisoners of war against another Iranian people, the Saki, but they turned against him. The Parthians were beaten and Phraates killed.

Antiochus XII waged war against the Arab people of the Nabataeans, who under the philhellene Aretas (86-62 BC) had taken Damascus. It was from this time that the infiltration of the Arabs into Syria began and the way was thus prepared for the victory of Islam. If it had not been for the victory of the Romans in 190, the Greeks of Asia would have offered greater resistance both to the Parthians of Persia and to the Arabs and other Semites.

The Seleucids were as a rule courageous rulers and fought for the Greek ideal of civilization, even if they were not granted the leisure to cultivate letters as the Ptolemies did.[28]

The Hellenization of Egypt

The position of the Greek language was still worse in Egypt, where the Ptolemies did not pursue the colonizing policy of

[28] See R. Grousset. *L'Empire du Levant*. 1946. pp. 30, 36, 40, 44.

the Seleucids. In Egypt, apart from Alexandria, which came to have a population of 500,000, the Ptolemies founded only a few cities—Ptolemais (Suakim), Bernice, Arsinoe, and others. All were small towns, and the military settlements such as Philadelphia, Panopolis, Lycopolis, Heliopolis, Letopolis, Cynopolis, Krocodilopolis and the rest, were smaller still. These latter towns were named after gods and were the capitals of the *nomes*, that is, of the military regions or administrative districts.

Of all the successors of Alexander the Great the Ptolemies alone cultivated letters and greatly promoted the cause of learning. This development was due to the School of Aristotle, from which came Demetrius of Phaleron, governor of Athens from 317 to 307 BC: it was Demetrius who recommended to Ptolemy I Lagus the founding of the Museum at Alexandria. The great libraries of Alexandria, the Museum and the Serapeum, were unique in the world.

Through the architect Deinocrates the Ptolemies made Alexandria the world's most beautiful city, laid out on a regular plan, with straight roads (following the old example of Hippodamus), gardens and harbours, with a wealth of statues and great buildings, and with an abundant supply of water which was procured by the link with the Nile. The two first Ptolemies with their famous sisters and consorts, Berenice and Arsinoe (who also gave their names to two small cities) fixed the outlines of the administration of Egypt. No large cities were founded but only small military stations or *cleruchies*, in which the land was given to Greek soldiers in return, of course, for military service. The papyri discovered over a great extent of Egypt show the distribution of Greeks throughout the country. At first the Egyptians were not made officials or soldiers, nor were they allowed to intermarry with the Greeks, even though it was impossible to prevent the scattered soldiery from intercourse with Egyptian women. From 200 BC, however,[29] Greeks ceased to come to Egypt in any numbers, intermarriage became commoner and use began to be made of Egyptians in the army and in the administration. Ptolemy VII Euergetes (145 BC) even persecuted Greek men of learning, who fled to Pergamon, and showed particular favour to the Egyptians. The eviction of the Greeks during the second cen-

[29] Tarn-Levy. *La Civilisation Hellénistique*. 1936. p. 184 ff.

tury BC weakened the dominion of the Ptolemies which was nearly subjugated by Antiochus IX Epiphanes. After the subjection of Egypt to the Romans (31 BC), the Greek element was again reinforced. It is even probable that if Cleopatra's lover, Antony, had won at Actium, he would have made Alexandria his capital.

In the economic sphere the Ptolemies followed the older system of the Pharaohs, entrusting the use of the land to the natives but retaining the lordship over it, always ready to confiscate the produce and in any case taking a large part of it throughout the country. They thus became the leading merchants, industrialists and bankers, since they had to sell the produce which they had accumulated, especially the corn and olive oil; they had to work up some of it — flax for instance — by an industrial process; and through the banks they had to handle the accounting and manage the intricate currency system of the Mediterranean world. They thus combined the monopolies of trade, industry and banking. The exploitation of the natives of course became unbearable and frequently provoked discontent and rebellion among the Egyptians; nevertheless, the Ptolemies assisted the development of large-scale commerce not only in the Mediterranean but also in the Red Sea [30] and the Indian Ocean. Sea routes to India and the coasts of east Africa were projected by Hippalus and the admiral Philo; at the same time various kinds of spice were already coming from these regions, the principal market for them being, eventually, Alexandria. As technique improved, Egypt itself became better cultivated, with the aid of new types of pump and other machines; new plants were also introduced where marshes had been drained or former tracts of desert irrigated by new cuttings to the Nile.

The development of trade and agriculture was the sole economic achievement of the Greeks in Egypt, which in many ways compensated for the hideous exploitation of the natives. It is true that it was only the earlier Ptolemies who led the way in economic development as also in the patronage of

[30] Agatharchides of Cnidos wrote a description of the Red Sea.

[31] Strabo (795) writes: "All the Ptolemies then, after the third, were corrupted by luxury and governed worse and worse; worst of all were the fourth Ptolemy and the seventh and last, the Flute-player" (the father of Cleopatra).

learning. The later Ptolemies with their family marriages, their dissolute manner of life [31] and their intestine struggles brought shame on their name in the pages of history.

The Balkan Peninsula

The Diadochi achieved far less in the way of colonization in the Balkan peninsula than in Egypt. Strictly speaking, only two cities were founded by Cassander, Cassandrea and the illustrious Thessalonike (Salonica). Antigonus Gonatas founded only one insignificant town, Antigonea, near Stobi in Macedonia. Just as the Greeks had from the first turned their eyes towards Asia and away from their ancient homeland the Balkans, so now the successors of Alexander who took control of Macedonia were much concerned with the inhabitants of Greece but never thought of applying the colonizing policy of the Seleucids to the Balkans. Had they done so, they might have extended the bounds of Greek civilization further to the north. But Alexander's own example was doomed to detach the Greeks from Europe and not merely to carry them into Asia but also to intermix them with a variety of peoples and, as it were, to adulterate them.[32]

If Greek influence had advanced northward, it would at once have surrounded the Illyrian kingdom of Agron whose political centre was in the neighborhood of Scutari and which not only dominated the Adriatic but had also occupied the more northerly of the Greek islands, Pharos (Hvar), Corcyra (Corfu) and others (except Issa [Hvis]), as well as the part of Epirus known as Atintania, and by doing so had made it easy to organize piratical raids as far as the Peloponnese.[33] Later on, perhaps, cooperation might have been successfully arranged between the Greeks and the Illyrians, and the crossing of the Romans into the Balkans in 220 BC and the subjugation of

[32] According to the historian Livy (38, 17): "The Macedonians who hold Alexandria in Egypt, Selencia and Babylon and other settlements scattered throughout the world, have degenerated into Syrians, Parthians and Egyptians."

[33] See K. Beloch. *Griechische Geschichte.* Vol. LV. 1. (2nd ed. 1925) p. 635. M. Holleaux. *Rome, la Grece et les Monarchies Helléinistiques au III siecle avant J. Christ,* 1935. p. 22. Agron's consort, Teuta, not only launched piratical expeditions against western Greece and the eastern coasts of Italy but also raids through the "pass of Antigonea," that is, the modern Klisura in Epirus.

the Illyrians might have been prevented. The subjection of
the Illyrians was the prologue to that of the Greeks. Indeed,
the great error of the Antigonids, an error which Philip would
certainly never have committed, was their shortsighted
Greek policy, which instead of carrying Greek civilization
northward, failed to attach the Illyrians to it, and failed to
defend it in alliance with the Illyrians, against the Roman
occupation. As it was, the conquest of Greece was made easy,
not merely because the Greeks had failed to cooperate with
the warlike Illyrian people and not merely because during
the third century BC they had pursued a petty policy of
purely Greek wars and internal feuds, but also because the
large number of settlements and new cities in Asia attracted
countless thousands of emigrants from Greece and diminished
the population of the country.[34] There are many evidences of
the depopulation of Greece, but it is enough to note here what
Dio Chrysostom writes in his "Euboean Discourse" [35] about
Euboea: "And now gentlemen," he says, "nearly two thirds
of our country (i.e. Euboea) are a desert through neglect
and depopulation, since now even the land at the city gates
is utterly uncultivated and terribly unsightly, as if it were
in the heart of some wilderness and not the suburbs of a city.
What lies inside the walls, on the other hand, is mostly sown
or grazed." From what follows the above passage it appears
that there was such a lack of farmers that if a cultivator were
found, he could farm other men's land free for ten years and
thereafter could merely pay part of his produce as rent.[36]

But the depopulation of Greece is also evident from the

---

[34] As Laurent says (*Essias d'Histoire Sociale. La Grece antique*. 1933. p.
167): "The result (of the emigrations) was the fall of Hellas proper, since
Asia caused the evacuation of Greece, just as America brought about the
fall of Spain and Portugal. In effect, economic activity followed the emigrants: from the ancient Greek cities they crossed over to Rhodes, Alexandria, Pergamon and Antioch in such numbers that the migratory movement
. . . finally beggared Greece and robbed it both of men and of economic
resources."

[35] Arnim's edition. Vol. I pp. 13, 31.

[36] Polybius likewise writes (XXXVII. 4): "In our own time the whole of
Greece is in the grip of childlessness, in other words of depopulation, which
has caused the cities to be left deserted and has resulted in dearth . . . ." Men
had families of one or two at most according to the same writer. And Strabo
speaks of the depopulation of Arcadia (388): ". . . for owing to the continual
wars cities which were formerly famous have been destroyed and those who

last stand of Corinth (146 BC), where the last of its commanders, Diaeus, had not sufficient freemen to repel the Romans
and was obliged to free the slaves in order to defend the
liberty of Greece with them! According to Polybius (XL, 2, 3),
"having sent to Megara and himself visited Argos, he wrote
to all the cities, bidding them free up to twelve thousand men
in the prime of life and to arm them and sent them to Corinth."
But a nation's freedom could not be saved by slaves and, since
he could not overcome the Romans, the gallant Diaeus committed suicide with his family, and the boorish Mummius, with
a relatively small army (30,000), not only took the wealthy
trading city of Corinth but destroyed it, in accordance with
the Roman system of extirpating a dangerous commercial rival
to the Roman plutocracy.

As Eduard Meyers says,[37] "Though Alexander's conquests
and the employment of thousands of men in the wars of the
Diadochi or in the founding of cities, old Hellas and Macedonia
lost their population."

Summary of Views on the Hellenishtic World

The Greek origin of the ancient Macedonians was disputed
by earlier investigators and by many enemies of Greece. Modern
scholars, including two Greek men of learning, George Hatzi-
dakis and Antonios Keramopoulos, are more disposed to admit
that the Macedonians were genuine Hellenes.[38] But irrespective
of this question of their authenticity as Greeks the services
rendered by Macedonia to Greek civilization and to the civilization of the world were unique and immeasurable. In the first
place, Macedonia was the bulwark of Greece which repulsed
the raids of the barbarians and prevented their descending
upon Hellas.[39]

Through the agency of Philip Macedonia united the Greek
world, and through Alexander it rendered a service to man-

---

worked the land have disappeared, even since the population of most of
the towns was concentrated in the so-called "Great City" (Megalopolis): so
now this "Great City" has suffered the fate predicted by the comic writers
and "the Great City is a great ruin."

[37] *Kleine Schriften*, 1 (1924), p. 231.

[38] Colin. *Rome et la Grece*. 1905. p. 74.

kind. Alexander was a disciple of the Macedonian Aristotle, one of the greatest intellects in the world's history, and under Aristotle's inspiration he took up the struggle against the barbarians, not with a view to their destruction as other conquerors did (including Caesar himself) but with a view to their civilization. The Greeks who pressed forward into Asia with Alexander were lost after his time, but their cultural influence was beyond calculation. The contact of Greek civilization with different peoples furthered their development and created new civilizations out of nothing. Islam itself is unthinkable without Alexander the Great, even though it became in the end, as Mommsen says, the executioner of Greek civilization. And what would Christianity have been without Hellenism, which bore witness on its behalf, wrote its defence, its literature and its history, warred against heresy, moulded its belief and developed its art? As Lietzman said, "It was through Hellenism that Christianity became a world religion."[40] Byzantium could never have survived for a thousand years in continuous conflict with the barbarians of Asia, if it had not been based upon the Greek communities of Asia Minor, as fortified by Alexander the Great and later ages.[41]

Greece then, through Alexander the Great, rendered services to the whole of humanity and to the whole history of the world. Nevertheless, these same Greeks who swarmed into Asia perished absolutely, some after a thousand years at the hands of the Semitic Arabs, who conquered Syria and Egypt, some in our own time after two and a half thousand years at the hands of the Turks in Asia Minor. To this day the Greek re-

[39] Polybius writes on this point (IX. 35): "How greatly the Macedonians deserve to be honoured, who for the greater part of their lives never ceased struggling with the barbarians on behalf of the security of the Greeks. Who does not know that Greek affairs would constantly have been in great peril, if we had not had as a protective outwork the Macedonians and the honourable pride of their kings? And here is the greatest proof of this. As soon as the Gauls came to despise the Macedonians after having defeated Ptolemy surnamed the Thunderbolt (Ceraunus), Brennus and his men at once disregarder the rest and invaded central Greece . . . a thing which would have happened many times before, had the Macedonians not been there to help."

[40] *Proceedings of the Academy of Athens*, Vol. XI (1936)) p. 249.

[41] Wileken. *Alexander der Grosse*. 1931. p. 304. See also Schaeder, *Die Antike*, 4,258.

mains in Syria show the cultural force of Hellenism and the decline which Semitic or Arab Mahommedanism brought upon that country. As Lietzman, who had travelled there, says,[42] "A journey through Syria as far as the Euphrates gives one a picture of the inexhaustible power of Greek civilization down in those regions."

Alexander died at Babylon when barely thirty-three years of age. There can be no doubt that if he had lived a few years longer, his vital energy would have led him westwards, and we can say that in that event the course of world history would have been other than it was. Instead of the destruction of so many Greek communities in Magna Graecia and in Hellas proper by Aemilius Paulus, Mummius, Sulla and many other designing Romans, those communities would have been used for civilizing ends. The Celtic race would not have been emasculated by Caesar but would have come under the influence of Greek civilization at an early stage and would have been able to stem the German invasions which brought so many disasters on the West. When the contact of Greek culture with remote Asiatic countries, such as Bactria, the modern Turkestan, and India, produced such beneficial results, we may imagine how swift would have been the development of the peoples of the West, the Gauls, the Spaniards, the Italians, the Germans and the peoples of North Africa; and who knows what splendours they might have conferred on the world? The Middle Ages would certainly not have come as they did.

It is true indeed that the Romans were forced to create a system of law in order to govern so many different peoples and that they felt the influence of Greece. Yet for all that they never ceased to be the jealous-minded shepherds and farmers of old Latium, spreading destruction and advancing their own cause by craft, and always by application of their "Divide and rule." The Romans continually borrowed from the Greeks the basic elements of civilization and where they could not borrow they destroyed, themselves proving barren and unproductive. "It is an indisputable fact," writes Vogt,[43] "that Roman literature is an imitation of Greek." According to Wilamowitz-Moellendorff,[44] "the history of the Italians is su-

[42] *Op. cit.* p. 248.

[43] *Römische Geschichte* 1932. p. 157

premely tragic, owing to the fact that they never seem to
have been able to master philosophy and science. This made
the collapse of ancient civilization inevitable." But the case
would have been otherwise if other peoples, the Gauls
above all, had come into contact with Greek civilization at
an earlier stage.

After what has been said above, we can understand how the
great sculptor Lysippus carved Alexander's statue as if he were
looking at Zeus and saying to him, "Zeus, I am making the
earth subject to me: you may keep Olympus." [45]

44 *Reden und Vorträge.* 2. 151.

45 Plutarch. *On Alexander's Fortune and Valour.* II. 3.

CHAPTER III

GREEK CIVILIZATION IN ASIA

The Greeks and the Idea of Law

The Greeks were the first people in the world to give a fuller development to the idea of Law and Justice,[46] since before them the will of the monarchs of the East had constituted Law, however arbitrary that will might be. The restless, freely enquiring Greek mind was the first to explore and adapt all the various forms of constitution from the monarchic and absolute (αἰσυμνῆται) to the communistic constitution of the Lipari Islands.[47] In each case local need soon led to the creation of the necessary constitutional forms — to military communism in Sparta, to democracy in Athens,

[46] Cf. J. Myres. *The Political Ideas of the Greeks*, 1927, pp. 98, 106 ff. And at a still later date only a Greek could have expressed himself as Dio Chrysostom did in his Seventy-Fifth Speech (Vol. II, p. 202 in Armin's edition): "Law is the guide of life, the impartial governor of cities and the measure of justice in affairs . . . without law no city can be administered. . . it is law which scours the sea and tames the land, law the very child of Zeus . . . and since Justice is a virgin it is Law alone whose chaste sobriety can keep her company." And the poet Sotades said: "Law is a god: reverence him always and at all times." (Diehl, *Anthologia Lyrica*. VI, p. 294). And Herodotus said of the Spartiates (VII, 104): ". . . for although they are free they are not altogether free, since the law is master over them."

[47] See Pöhlmann. *Fr. Oertal Geschichte der Sozialen Frage und des Sozialismus in der Antiken Welt*, 3rd ed. Vol. I (1925), p. 36. According to Diodorus Siculus V, 9.: "Later on, in the course of their wars against the Tyrrhenians who were ravaging their coasts, (the inhabitants of the Lipari islands) built a fleet and dividing themselves into two bodies, some worked the land, treating the islands as common property, while others took the field against the pirates; and they continued to live communally for some time, pooling their resources and living in communal messes." The necessities of defence forced the Greeks of the Lipari Islands to unite against their enemies and just as the spoils of victory were held in common, so the whole of their territory became a common possession. It was in this way that the communism of the Lipari islanders came into being.

and so on. In city after city it is amazing to see the variety
of constitutional and political forms which the Greek mind
evolved for the government of peoples. A philosopher like
Plato investigated not only the origin of the world but also
the best method of governing states and finally arrived at
a conception of extreme communistic rule and of a war
to the death against the individualism which had found such
a fertile soil in Greece.[48] Aristotle's *Politics* is one of the most
useful books ever composed by man, precisely because
Aristotle set down in it the whole variety of the conclusions
of the Greek mind on the problems of human government.

The Greeks were the first people in the world to
realize the nature of social problems and to react to the problem of social injustice, even though they did not of course
provide a final solution to these questions.[49] The Greeks
merely formulated these problems[50] and showed their extreme difficulty by their attempts to solve them. The Greeks
might admire the grandeur of Plato's philosophy or the
justice of Aristides; yet there still remained the miserable Penestae in Thessaly, the even more miserable Helots
in a gallant Sparta, the Mnoites and Aphamiotes or Klarotes
in Crete, the equally wretched Mariandyni[51] in the Pontic
Heraclea, the Hectemori in ancient Attica, and others beside
Solon's "Seisachtheia" and his land reforms show the boldness
and resource of the Greek mind but they did not provide the de-

---

[48] I need only quote the passage in Aristotle's *Politics* II, 9.8: "The
special doctrine of Phaleas (of Chalcedon) is the equal distribution of
property: and the institution of community messes for women . . ."

[49] One must of course condemn the unlimited employment of slave labour
in Greece. The sole extenuating feature is that these slaves, who were
bought cheaply on the Black Sea coast, in Asia Minor and elsewhere, lived
such impoverished and wretched lives in their homelands that they themselves preferred slavery in Greece which in no case made their situation
worse and often made it better.

[50] It has been rightly said that, "The value of Greek social theory is permanent: it demonstrated to us that the happiness of people depends not
so much on the production of the greatest possible mass of goods but far
more on the justice of their distribution." (Pöhlmann. *Oertal, op. cit.* I,
480).

[51] Strabo. 542. "The Milesians, who first founded Heraclea, reduced to
slavery the Mariandyni who originally inhabited the place: indeed they
were sold as slaves by them . . . just as the so-called Mnoan community
were made serfs to the Cretans and the Penestae to the Thessalians."

sired solution even in Attica, let alone in other similar cases in ancient Greece. As Laurent remarks, "The Greeks knew the social struggle in all its forms, as is proved by the fact that in the course of twenty-four centuries none of the generations which have lived since' the Greeks have added anything to their observations." [52] In general it may be said that it was in ancient Greece that the cleavage between the individual and the community was first realized and one might add that the ancient world was overthrown in the middle of its struggle to bridge this cleavage.

Worship and Deifnation of the Kings

Everything which has been said above regarding political and social questions refers to the European Greeks. When the Greeks invaded Asia they were to rule in accordance with native tradition and with the disregard of human feeling to which they were condemned by the theocratic conception of the supreme ruler. Ever since he had entered Asia Minor, but especially after his invasion of Egypt, Alexander the Great had begun to consider how he was to govern his foreign subjects; he had wished, like the Pharaohs, to be a king by divine dispensation; he meant, even, to be the son of Zeus and a little later a god in his own right. On this basis the peoples would submit blindly to him and he would rule them without trouble. In Bactria he imposed on non-Greeks the adoration (προσκύνησις) ' of his person but did not venture to require it of the Greeks as well. Kaerst [53] suspects from this that the "Alexandreia", which according to Strabo were celebrated by the river Teos, were appointed as a religious festival while Alxander was still alive.

However this may be, the Greek kings of the East were familiarized, by Alexander's example, with the idea of deifi-

---

[52] J. Laurent. *Essais d'Histoire Sociale. La Grece Antique.* 1923, p. 23.

[53] J. Kaerst. *Geschichte des Hellenismus.* Vol. I. 3rd ed. (1927), p. 345. Strabo (644) writes: "There lies above Chalcis a grove dedicated to Alexander the son of Philip and games called the Alexandreia are proclaimed by the general assembly of the Ionians and celebrated there. An inscription even places Philip V among the gods: 'Alcaeus, son of Heracleides, to Serapis, Isis and King Philip." (*Bull Correspondance Hellénique*, Vol. XVIII (1894), p. 417).

cation(as in the case of the Ptolemies) or to that of elevation after death to the status of "hero" (as in the case of the Seleucids and Attalids). This latter was a Greek practice, a reward to those who had undertaken superhuman labours on behalf of mankind when they were on earth. Only the successors of Alexander in Greece, the Antigonids, never sought, and indeed could not have sought, deification from the Greeks.

Elevation to the status of hero — that is to say, the kind of heroic worship accorded by the Greeks to Achilles, Brasidas, Aratus and many others, as local or national "heroes" and founders of cities — could easily be introduced into Asia too, as a posthumous honour, without offending Greek ideas. What was repugnant to the Greek mind was the deification of the ruler in Egypt while he was still alive, although by the Oriental, accustomed to theocratic rule, this was regarded as essential. The Greeks were equally repelled by the practice of attaching to rulers even after death the names of Greek gods. Thus Seleucus I was after his death entitled Zeus, Antiochus I Apollo, and so on.

A religious significance attached to names such as Soter (Saxior), Epiphanes (Manifest, Illustrious), Euergetes (Benefactor), which were bestowed on various Seleucid rulers and others. The name Soter, like the feast of Epiphany, later passed to Christianity.

Country and Town

The Greek kings of the East were lords of the soil and wealth of their countries, granting the use of them at will to cities or individuals. In Egypt, consequently, the possessions of the Crown were enormous, as also were the possessions of the temples both there and in Asia Minor. The estates of the temples of Comani and Pessinus in Asia Minor were cultivated by the forced labour of temple slaves, numbering thousands; [54] those of the temple of Isis at Philae in Egypt were similarly cultivated.

The "royal lands" were worked by the "people" (λαοί), that is to say by labourers who were to some extent serfs in

[54] P. Jouguet. *L'Impérialisme macédonien et l'Hellénisation de l'Orient,* 1926, p. 418.

so far as they were obliged to work on the royal estates for a
certain specified period.[55] In Egypt, however, there
were also freemen who were agricultural specialists and
were used for the more difficult types of agriculture such as
papyrus-growing. To those who undertook military duties the
so-called "cleruchies" were allotted, but after the soldier's
death this land could be bestowed on another. The lesser
military colonies were also called "settlements" (κατοικίαι).
The towns, as we have said, were inhabited by Greeks and
consequently received from the rulers various privileges, which
the latter might also withdraw. The inhabitants of Alexandria
were, in addition, granted exemption from military service;
while the Jews of Alexandria were allowed to administer themselves according to the law of their religion. The Greeks
in the cities, therefore, enjoyed autonomy and were consequently governed in accordance with the traditions of ancient
Greece, with popular assemblies and Councils and other Greek
institutions. In some cases cities enjoyed exemption from taxes
and contributions. Gymnasia, theatres and baths were to be
found in them and, in general, the ancient Greek way of life [56]
was cultivated with some sense of superiority amid foreign surroundings. In Egypt particularly, the posts of Gymnasiarch, or
President of the Games, was a most honorable one for a family
to hold.

Apart from the cities, the Greek kings found invaluable support in the Greek bureaucracy and in the army, which likewise consisted mainly of Greek officers and soldiers. On this
basis the successors of Alexander, following his policy of racial
rapprochement, but relying chiefly on Greeks as city settlers,
soldiers and officials, were able to rule the East for about two
centuries (the Attalids, however, only during the period 283-
133 BC) and Rome, thereafter, largely followed their method
of government.

Economic Development

Up to Alexander's conquest of Asia economic life and
the trade of Greece had circulated within the Mediterran-

55 G. Glotz. *Le Travail dans la Grece Ancienne.* Paris 1920, pp. 408 ff.

56 W. Otto. *Kulturgeschichte des Altertums,* 1925, p. 97.

ean Sea and the Black Sea, and even this with certain limitations in so far as the Carthaginians and Phoenicians opposed it. After the conquest of Asia the Greeks expanded the whole of their economic life and extended their trade as far as India and Turkestan. The Seleucids made a military expedition to the Persian Gulf, which also discharged commercial tasks, and the Ptolemies founded trading stations—Berenice and others—on the Red Sea, and linked them up by canals with the Nile and Alexandria in order to facilitate trade with East Africa and Arabia. The famous Hippalus, precursor of Vasco da Gama, discovered the periodic winds of the Indian Ocean—the monsoons—and thus assisted navigation as far as Ceylon; and the admiral Philo explored the coasts of East Africa. A complete monetary system was introduced into Egypt for the first time— a necessity in view of the huge commerce of that country; coins of the Ptolemies and other successor kings are found in the depths of Asia as far as Tibet.

Large-scale trade was also helped by the development of agriculture. In their poverty-stricken native Greece, the Greeks had made no effort to perfect their agricultural methods by mechanical or other means. On the contrary, they had left agriculture mainly in the hands of slaves, Helots, Penestae and other serfs who had neither the will nor the ability to do their work thoroughly. In the Seleucid kingdom, however, and still more in Egypt they devoted more attention to the state of agriculture, which in those countries was capable of yielding them profits. As a result, the Greeks were the first to improve agriculture there by the introduction of the hydraulic works or mechanical devices (dredges, windmills and watermills), which they invented at this time. Lake Mareotis was drained and put under cultivation, as also was the province of Arsinoe, the modern district of Fayoum. Similarly, the Seleucids drained the region of the River Chrysorrhoas near Damascus and made it available for cultivation.[57] Certain regions of Syria (the Orontes valley, the country between Emesa and Palmyra, and others) which were desert during the period of Turkish rule contained a large number of towns in the time of the Seleucids

57 J. Toutain. *L'Economie Antique,* 1927, pp. 107, 119, 126, 130, 152, 215 and ff.

and must consequently have been under cultivation.

The Greeks introduced the vine into the East, even as far east as Susiana, and also into Egypt, where they further cultivated the olive and instituted, in particular, the oil monopoly. Through their monopolies the Ptolemies regulated the quantity and the price of certain specified products, without the other restrictions which we find later on in Roman times (for example, the veto on the cultivation of silphium). Generally speaking, the whole banking and credit system reached a high state of development in Egypt.[58] Further, while introducing new agricultural methods in Asia and Egypt, the Greeks, conversely, transplanted from Asia the peach, the damson and various kinds of terebinth. Many other plants were later introduced via Greece into Italy[59] as the olive had formerly been — damsons, almonds, chestnuts, peaches, walnuts, etc.

In Egypt the Ptolemies developed a great navy and constructed the largest and most efficient ships of antiquity, the like of which even the later Middle Ages did not know. In Egypt too they built on the island of Pharos the lighthouse of that name with the celebrated inscription:

Sostratus, son of Dexiphanes, the Cnidian

to the divine Soters,

in aid of mariners.

Rhodes

Among the older Greek states, Rhodes had expanded greatly up till the creation of the free port of Delos (166 BC). Owing to its situation and to its skilful policy it had succeeded in developing a considerable trade and it had been the first state of antiquity to develop maritime law; it had, moreover, rendered

---

[58] See A. Andreades.. *Works*, Vol. I (1938), p. 365; J. Desvernois. "Banques te Banquiers dans l'Egypt Ancienne sous les Ptolémees et la Domination Romaine," in *Bulletin de la Société Royale d'Archéologie d'Alexandrie*, No. 23 (1928), p. 303.

[59] See V. Hehn. *Kulturpflanzen und Hanstieve in ihrem übergang aus Asien nach Griechenland und Italien, sowie in das übrige Europa*, 8th ed. by O. Schrader, 1911, p. 122 ff. According to Hehn wine too was introduced into Italy by the Greeks *(op. cit.* p. 71)

great services in the Mediterranean by its fight against piracy.[60]

Rhodes possessed an aristocratic constitution, but its government consisted of men of affairs, merchants and sailors who
knew the value of labour and therefore made provisions for
indigent workers. According to Strabo (652) : "The Rhodians
have a sense of social welfare, even though they are not a
democracy, since they wish to keep together in unity the mass
of the poor. The people are therefore fed, and by national
custom the well-to-do support the needy..." Rhodes came to
be popular throughout Greece and in consequence, when it
suffered from the great earthquake of 227 BC, generous help
came in from all sides.

Through the activity of the Greeks in Asia and Egypt economic life attained for the first time a development unknown
in the ancient world. Certainly one cannot claim that the lot
of their native subjects was invariably happy: both as conquerors and as rulers the Greeks exploited the natives to
the highest degree, with the result that in Egypt native risings
took place with Nubian assistance, such as cannot readily be
paralleled before the organization of the Ptolemaic state.[61] But
in spite of this these populations led in every way a better life
under Greek rule than they had formerly under their native
kings.

Greece

While, however, the Greeks were prospering and expanding
in Asia, in Old Greece, from the third century on, a decline
set in which was economic as well as political and cultural.
The multiplication of emigrants to Asia caused a reduction in
the population[62] of Old Greece with a reduction in the number
of agricultural labourers and the consequent abandonment of
much of the land. A great many properties were sold, because
their owners wished to leave, and in this way large estates

[60] See the article "Rhodos," in *Pauly-Wissowa Realencyclopädie;* M.
Rostovtseff "Rhodes, Delos and Hellenis fic. Commerce." *The Cambridge
Ancient History,* Vol. VIII (1930), p. 619.

[61] Cf. P. Jouguet, *L'Impérialisme Macédonien et l'Hellénisation de l'Orient,*
1926, p. 387.

[62] Besides emigration and civil war, malarial fever helped to reduce the
population of European Greece.

(*latifundia*) were created and this great inequality in the distribution of property had important effects on the social situation. In Sparta Agis and Cleomenes tried vainly in the third century BC, to restore some equality of proportion between private property and the rest of the community by the redistribution of land. Many cities bought corn for distribution to the poor. In the struggle against the Romans the discontented poorer Greeks fought without enthusiasm. Later, at the time of the massacre of the Romans (88 BC), many wealthy Greeks were massacred as well, although the fighting was mainly against the Romans.

Emigration to Asia, then, caused a deterioration in the economic and social condition of Old Greece [63] as well as causing a reduction in the population as mentioned above.

Cultural Development

An eternal debt of gratitude is owed to the great historian Johann Droysen [64] who discovered, so to speak, the Greek achievement from the time of Alexander onwards and gave the name of *Hellenismus* to the Hellenistic era, in contradistinction to the earlier *Hellenentum*, defining it in a way which admitted of no question and which freed scholarship from earlier preconceptions. The Hellenistic era is astonishing in its fertility and originality, above all in the sphere of knowledge, which the dispersal of the Greek race was powerless to affect. A brief survey of the cultural and artistic activity of the Greeks from the time of Alexander the Great down to the time of Christ will make their achievement clear.

It must be observed at once that the centre of cultural activity shifts gradually from Old Greece to Asia and Egypt. Consequently, while creative minds steadily grow fewer in Europe, in Asia and Egypt they increase in number both before the Christian era and for some centuries after, as we shall see later. A fundamental change takes place in the first century BC, when mysticism comes to exert a radical influence on the rationalistic way of thought and the original outlook of the Greek mind.

63 In C. Barbagallo's book, *Le Déclin d'une Civilisation ou la Fin de la Grece Antique.* 1927, the decline of Old Greece is depicted in too startling colours without any reference or comparison to Greek expansion in Asia.

64 J. Droysen. *Geschichte des Hellenismus,* Vols. I & II (1836-43).

Here attention may be drawn to the general observation made by Wilamowitz-Moellendorf [65] which applies also to cultural activity: "In the four generations from Alexander down to Antiochus the Great and from Aristotle down to Eratosthenes the Greek people produced a prodigious number of outstanding men, so that their later falling off may perhaps be considered inevitable . . . . The age of Caesar cannot show in any field of activity a single even moderately outstanding Greek." During the period from about 320-290 BC, within a space of three decades, new philosophical systems were built up in an astounding rivalry of creative minds — the Stoic philosophy of Zeno, the philosophy of Epicurus, not to mention the Academy of Arcesilaus (315-241) and the Aristotelian school of Theophrastus. The founders of these schools were not from Old Greece but their creative work was done in Athens, since it was there that Socrates, Plato, the Sophists and Aristotle had preceded them. Epicurus was from Samos (341-270), Arcesilaus from the Aeolid of Asia Minor, Theophrastus from Lesbos (374-286), Zeno from Kition in Cyprus and in fact of Semitic origin. The cosmopolitan [66] character of the Stoic philosophy is partly attributable to Zeno's native country which permitted him a closer knowledge of the East and of the situation created there by Alexander's new policy. The king of Macedonia, Antigonus Gonatas, was also a disciple and supporter of Zeno, and his two most zealous disciples were from the East, Cleanthes from Assos in the Aeolid and Chrysippus from Soli in Cilicia. Panaetius, who taught the Romans the Stoic philosophy (180-110), was a Rhodian, whom Cicero followed in his philosophical treatise on Duty (*De Officiis*). The Roman emperor Marcus Aurelius was also a Stoic. The Stoic philosophy despised matter and looked on "virtue" as its master aim. "Conscience and duty were the foundation

---

[65] *Die Griechische Literatur des Altertums (Kultur der Gegenwart* I, VIII 1905) p. 82. A. Cronet, however, says that the three centuries from 300 BC to Augustus, "ont fait de la culture grecque le patrimoine commun de toutes les nations civilisées." *L'Hellénisation du monde antique*, 1914, p. 275)

[66] Cf. the words of the sophist Antiphon: "In nature . . . we are all born alike, barbarians and Greeks . . . We all breathe in the air through our mouths and noses . . . " *(The Oxyrrhynchus Papyri*, Vol. II, 1915. No. 1364).

stones of Stoic morals. The influence of Stoicism on the ancient world and on Christianity was great. The Stoic philosophy was at the same time a religion." [67]

The last of the great philosophers, the second Aristotle of antiquity, Posidonius, from Apamea in Syria (135-51 BC), was a Syrian, according to Reinhardt [68] who rediscovered him. Posidonius, he says, "stands in his own right on a level with Aristotle and Chrysippus as a philosopher and as a systematic thinker" — but according to Wilamowitz — Moellendorff [69] he was a Greek. Posidonius travelled more widely than any other ancient explorer and worked in his second homeland, Rhodes, which was also the centre where Hipparchus and Dionysius Thrax worked. The wide learning and selective mind of Posidonius —he was a pupil of Panaetius — unfortunately did not prevent his falling under the influence of Chaldaean astrology and oriental mysticism and thus contributing to the force of their impact. As a result the last of the philosophic systems, those of the Neopythagoreans and the Neoplatonists, could not fail to be influenced by the mysticism of the East and to take on a theological complexion. According to Schaeder [70] Posidonius was also influenced by Manicheism. Wilamowitz-Moellendorff, on the other hand, considers that "Posidonius is the last great thinker of Greece, just as Rhodes is the last citadel of Greek freedom and learning."

It remains to add that Carthage too produced a philosopher, Hasdrubal who changed his name to Cleitomachus, the prolific pupil of Carneades of Cyrene.

During the third century BC the spirit of Old Greece was by no means extinct. Athens gave birth to the great comic poet Menander (342-291 BC) whose realistic comedy of manners later, through the Latin writers Plautus and Terence (who imitated him and translated some of his works), influenced the Spanish dramatist Calderon, Shakespeare and Molière.

---

[67] Tarn-Lévy. *La Civilisation Hellénistique.* p. 312.

[68] K. Reinhardt. *Poseidonios.* 1921, p. 4.

[69] *Der Glaube der Hellenen.* Vol. II (1932), p. 402. Dessau also considers Posidonius to have been a Greek and treats with sarcasm those who would have him of Semitic origin. *(Geschichte der römischen Kaiserzeit,* Vol. II. 2, 624).

[70] *Die Antike,* 4, 256.

Menander's literary style was followed by a great number of excellent poets (Philemon, Diphilus, Posidippus and others), whose works unfortunately have not survived, but Menander's "New Comedy" may be regarded as the last great poetic achievement of Athens.

Old Greece produced one more great historian, Polybius of Megalopolis (205-125 BC), who was the first to write general history with a philosophical commentary and a more scientific handling of his sources and his aids. Polybius knew Italy and was concerned with universal (world) history, regarding it as "the best of educations" and the experience to be gathered from it as highly instructive. In his words (III 31.12), "If one takes away from history the questions why, how and to what end a given thing was done . . . what is left may be a prize essay but it is not instructive. It may give pleasure for the moment, but it is quite unprofitable for the future." It is worth noting that Polybius was the first historian to attach great significance to geographical environment or to the natural surroundings and their influence on man (III. 36.6, and IV. 21.1.) He was the better able to observe the power of physical environment in that he accompanied Roman generals to Africa and Italy, as well as to Greece.

Literature

After the Greek school of Menander and Polybius we must turn to Egypt, where Greek supremacy and prosperity were bound to express themselves in a rich flowering of the arts. The first thing to be noted is the greatest and the most valuable of the Ptolemaic achievements in Egypt. On the advice and under the guidance of Demetrius of Phaleron, the first of the Ptolemies, the son of Lagus, founded at Alexandria the first great library and the first proper university under the name of the Museum or Temple of the Muses, whose priest directed the famous foundation. The Museum was situated in the great complex of buildings which also contained the palace of the Ptolemies. Strabo (794) writes: "The Museum is also part of the palace: it consists of a cloister, a hall and a large building containing the refectory of the scholars who form the staff of the Museum. This body has its own finances and a priest who is in charge of the Museum." The philosophers who took their name from the institution and the scholars who lived there permanently and were supported by it as research workers and teachers formed a religious community, in conformity with the character of the foundation. The Athenaeum founded by Hadrian at Rome was a direct copy of the Museum. The first museum in the modern sense of the word, namely a collection of works of art, was formed at Pergamon, where a library was also established on the Alexandrian model. The Museum at Alexandria helped to set the modern world an example of scholarship which was the principal achievement of the Hellenistic age, whereas poetry, drama, philosophy and fine art had been the main achievement of the Ionians of Asia Minor and Attica. The collection and arrangement of books, the collation and copying of the Homeric and other poems gave rise to the world's first systematic study of literature, that is to say the criticism and interpretation of literary texts. Similarly the study of texts gave rise to the first European grammar (the Indians did indeed produce grammatical works before the Greeks but these were still unknown in Europe), which as a work of higher abstract thought, was made possible by the aid of the Stoic philosophy. The Romans copied Greek grammatical studies closely. One of the first literary scholars was the conscientious Callimachus ("no poetry," he said, "without proof"), who was also a respectable poet, although he drew his inspiration more from books than from life. He composed elegies and epigrams with a great deal of technical skill and concision, avoiding lengthy epigrams. His best known poems are the "Causes," the "Lock of Berenice," and the "Arsinoe," in which he laments the death, and the apotheosis, of Ptolemy the Second's great queen and sister. Generally speaking, the poetry of Callimachus was profuse in flattery of the Ptolemies. One of his exquisite epigrams may be quoted here:

"Here Saon of Acanthus, Dicon's son, rests in holy
sleep: say not that the good die." [71]

Besides Callimachus, philosopher, scholar and poet, Alexandria formed three other great literary scholars, Aristophanes

[71] On Callimachus see C. Trypanis. *Alexandrian Poetry* (in Greek) Vol. I. (1943), p. 79 ff. Callimachus lived about 310-240 BC; he was a grandson of Callimachus the general.

of Byzantium (247-180 BC), Zenodotus of Ephesus (d. 260) and the greatest scholar of all, Aristarchus the Alexandrian, "by descent a Samothracian" (217-145 BC). The creation of the great Library of the Ptolemies and of the world's first school of literary studies was an invaluable service to mankind, since it preserved the works of classical antiquity and set the world the example of literary scholarship.

Mathematics

Besides literature, mathematical science was also strengthened and developed to a remarkable degree. According to Metzner,[72] "In the history of mathematical science there is only one other period of about 200 years which can be compared for productivity to the period from 300 to 200 BC and may even excel it, namely the period from Kepler to Gauss (1600-1850 AD)." The earliest and greatest of the Greek mathematicians, astronomers and engineers lived in the third century BC. Euclid systematized mathematical knowledge up to his time and in his "Elements," which are indispensable even today, he laid the foundation for the development of mathematics, and particularly of geometry. Archimedes of Syracuse (280-214) was the founder of the science of engineering. Apollonius of Perga in Pamphylia, the "great geometer," wrote on elementary conics and was the inventor of trigonometry. Archimedes and Apollonius of Perga were the greatest of the Greek mathematicians. Aristarchus of Samos was the Copernicus of antiquity; he was the first to teach that the earth moved round the sun. His observations were forgotten by mankind and had to be discovered anew by Copernicus in modern times. Eratosthenes of Cyrene (272-195) was a pupil of Ariston the Chian and was the founder of scientific geography and chronology: he was the first to measure, at Syene in Egypt, the circumference of the earth, and he drafted the first map.[73] Hipparchus, of Nicaea in Bithynia (190-120 BC), taught at Rhodes and discovered hundreds of stars, as well as the use of trigonometry

---

[72] K. Metzner. "Apollonius von Perge im Rahmen des grossen Jahrhundertes Griechischer Mathematik (300-200 BC)", in *Neue Jahrbücher für Wissenschaft und Jugendbildung*, Vol. VI (1930), p. 474.

[73] On Eratosthenes, see E. Schwarz. *Charakterköpfe aus der antiken Literatur*, Vol. II (1920), p.86.

in astronomical calculation. He and Aristarchus are the two greatest Greek astronomers. Among other engineers should be noted Ctesibius and the hydraulic engineer Heron of Alexandria who recognized the possibilities of steam, air and water power and constructed steam turbines, pumps and engines: unfortunately not all his works have survived.

Medicine

In addition to literature and mathematics the Museum also greatly helped the advancement of medical knowledge. The Ptolemies allowed medical men to examine corpses (and even, according to rumour, living criminals), and it thus became possible for Herophilus, a doctor from Chalcedon, to lay the foundations of anatomy, to describe the pancreas and other organs of the body and to conduct the first study of the human nerves: he was also the first to observe the circulation of the blood, which was subsequently rediscovered by Harvey. Erasistratus, a doctor from Kea, was the first to succeed in distinguishing the motor from the sensory nerves, to describe the convolutions of the brain and the cerebellum and to attempt a number of difficult experiments.[74] Herophilus and Erasistratus created medical schools called after their own names: Philinus of Kea was likewise a notable physician.

Navigators and Explorers

Among the geographers and explorers of the Hellenistic age we must note, besides Nearchus (who in Alexander's time coasted from India to the Persian Gulf) and Hippalus (the discoverer of the monsoons), Megasthenes who on the orders of Seleucus I went as envoy to India and described that country in his "Indica." Again at the bidding of Seleucus, the admiral Patrocles explored the Caspian Sea, while at the command of Ptolemy II Euergetes (283-245) Eudoxus of Cyzicus made a voyage to India and subsequently sailed along a part of the African coast south of Ethiopia.

[74] A Kouzis. *History of Medicine* (in Greek) Vol. I (1929), p. 166 ff.; A. Kouzis. "The Contribution of Ancient Greek Science to the Foundation of Medicine," in *Proceedings of the Academy of Athens*, Vol. VII (1932), p. 116 (in Greek)

Poetry

Apart from the "New Comedy" of Menander and his successors, poetry was practiced outside Greece proper and was primarily lyrical. Euripides may be regarded as the father of this poetry since it was he who first introduced the erotic, and romantic element. Antimachus of Colophon may also be considered as a forerunner, the writer of the famous elegy to his mistress, Lyde. One of the first elegiac poets was Philetas of Cos, to whom his fellow-citizens erected a bronze statue after his death. Besides the learned poet Callimachus, Theocritus of Syracuse also lived at Alexandria. Theocritus is principally known as the writer par excellence of pastoral poetry, but in addition he composed a number of epigrams and other poems and was one of the most prolific and most original writers of antiquity. In Hellenistic times a good deal of light poetry was written in the form of the mime, which was considerably older as a literary creation but had not had any very wide extension. Of the new poets in this genre the most considerable was Herondas of Cos, whose iambic mimes were discovered, written on papyrus, in 1891. The writers of mimes, idylls and epigrams drew from life, in contrast, as we have noted, to Callimachus, who drew largely from books. The dissolute life of Alexandria was portrayed by the poet Sotades, whose outspokenness led to his suicide. The Syrian epigrammatist, Meleager of Gadara was a cosmopolitan and did not hesitate to avow it; many other poets, besides, wrote excellent epigrams, such as Leonidas of Tarentum, Asclepiades of Samos — both of an earlier generation — and others.

Alexandrian poetry had a great effect on Rome (Callimachus's "Lock", for example, was translated by the Roman poet Catullus) and through Rome on the rest of the world.

Foreigners Writing in Greek

One feature of the Hellenistic age and of its cosmopolitan outlook was that many foreigners wrote in Greek without being intellectually Hellenized. Thus the Egyptian priest Manetho wrote a history of Egypt, based on the hieroglyphic inscriptions, and the Babylonian priest Berosus wrote on Babylon and transmitted the astrological lore of Chaldeans. These two

foreign scholars flourished during the first half of the third
century BC. Similarly — but later — in the first century AD
—came the Jewish authors. Philo of Alexandria and Josephus
of Jerusalem, the first of whom endeavored to reconcile the
Old Testament with Greek thought. No less typical was the
translation of the Septuagint (the "Seventy") made at Alexandria at the instance of the Jews there, who had learnt Greek,
while in Judaea the language was Aramaic.

The power of the Greek language in Egypt is clearly shown,
again, by the number of Greek words in Coptic liturgical texts.

"Asianism" and "Atticism"

The prodigious extension of Greek civilization by Alexander made it necessary to have a single common language and
this, with some necessary modifications, the Attic dialect of
Greek became, since up to this time it was in Attic that the majority of the creations of the Greek mind, and the greatest
variety of them, had been written. The ascendancy of the
Koine (the "common tongue") caused the ancient dialects of
Greece to be superseded by degrees and they practically ceased
to exist. In the time of Hegesius of Magnesia, by Mount Sipylus,
this Koine, or common dialect, began to be written in an over-
emphatic and excessively rhetorical style, and from this it earn-
ed the name of "Asian" (Strabo speaks of "Asian flamboyance"). This Asianism[75] in language, which to some extent appeared in Rhodian art — provoked a reaction and a longing
for a return to the finer style of the ancient classics; it gave
rise in fact to Atticism or archaism — in art as well as
letters — from the first century BC, even in Rome itself, where
Dionysius of Halicarnassus, one of its main initiators and the
writer of the "Roman Archaeology", was living in the time of
Augustus.

The prevalence of Atticism, or archaism, had terrible consequences for the history of Greek literature. While it proved
quite unable to suppress the inflated style of Asianism, it
caused all works not written in the Attic dialect to be mercilessly hunted down and an enormous number of them to be

[75] U. Wilamowitz-Moellendorff. "Asianismus und Attizismus," in *Hermes*.
Vol. XXXV (1900), p. 1 ff.

destroyed. Even apart from this, being confined within the narrow limits of antiquity, it despised the language of its own time and shrank from writing it, although the common tongue had no connection whatever with Asianism. In this way Atticism created a permanent gulf between the written language and that currently spoken. From time to time works were written in the vulgar speech, as indeed the Gospels themselves were, but the power of Atticism was such that not even the language of the Gospels was able to impose itself and to break the power of archaism. And in the fourth century AD, when the new Greek language had taken firmer shape, with all its characteristics, its abandonment of ancient prosody and the rest, the archaizers took no notice but continued to denounce everything that was not Attic. In short, although Atticism had originally been a reaction against an affected style, it gradually became perverted and began to make war on all literary forms that were not Attic, while the bombastic style was tolerated so long as it was combined with Attic usage.

Fine Arts in the Hellenistic World [76]

In the fine arts also the Hellenistic age could point to not a few achievements of credit. After the example of the architect Deinocrates, the builder of Alexandria, the Hellenistic cities adopted, for the most part, a fixed design with a regular street-plan. Thus, a definite urban style was created, carrying to its conclusion the work of the earlier master, Hippodamus. Further, architecture borrowed from the East new elements such as the dome and the curve, and gave birth to a new style which had no need for a blind imitation of the older Greek art. The basic features of Greek architecture in the Hellenistic age, with special reference to large constructions such as porticoes, libraries, squares and propylaea, are set out in the work of the Roman Vitruvius. From the fourth century BC onwards there begins likewise the spread of coloured tesselated work and mosaic in temples and other large buildings. The Romans too made use of this art, but it was the Byzantines who brought it to its greatest perfection and extended its use to sacred pictures.

[76] See H. Tsountas. *History of Ancient Greek Art*, (in Greek) 1928.

Sculpture and painting showed a new vigorous development. In Egypt these two arts devoted close attention to life and depicted it realistically without the idealization of an earlier age. Art also discovered "the power of ugliness"as Rodenwaldt said. An ugly old woman, for instance, could now be portrayed by a painter or sculptor in Alexandria, while at an earlier date, in the fourth or fifth century BC, this had been rare (cp. however, the Drunk Old Woman of Myron). Only Alexandrian art was capable of representing Homer as blind. The Roman art of realistic portraiture must have followed in the footsteps of Alexandria.

From the realistic conception of art it was an easy step for artists to *genre,* and particularly to the sympathetic portraiture of children. In the second century BC the sculptor Boethus made his Child struggling with a Goose and other artists chose similar subjects.

But Alexandrian art did not confine itself to portraying the man in the street and different racial types such as Negroes, or to portraiture of a realistic kind for its own sake. It introduced into sculpture, and perfected in painting, the art of landscape, which was among its most important successes. In painting, too, the portraits found with the mummies of the Fayoum ought not to be forgotten, nor the painter Antiphilus, celebrated for *genre* and caricature.[77] The Greek Christian art of the catacombs, with its flowers and birds and its various symbols, and the art of the mosaics, are likewise of high importance.

It must be noted, further, that Greek artists undertook in Egypt the task of raising to a higher level the representations of the gods, just as the artists of the fifth century had done in Greece. Thus the sculptor Bryaxis, a pupil of Scopas, made a statue of the god Sarapis after the model of the Zeus of Pheidias, and Isis was assimilated to the goddess Demeter.

In Rhodes and Pergamon art followed a different course. The statue of Laocoon, which later won the admiration of Lessing and the archaeologists of an earlier generation, was typical both in its massive conception and in the vividness of

[77] Antiphilus was the latest of the great painters of Asia Minor, after Parrhasius of Ephesus, Apelles of Colophon and Protogenes, a native of Caunus in Caria who flourished at Rhodes.

its emotion. In Pergamon, the Battle of the Giants on the great Altar of Zeus is likewise distinguished by its vivid renderings of mental feeling and the representation of emotion and conflict which the sculptor has striven to achieve in correspondence with his subject. The famous statues which were set up in memory of the victory of the Attalids over the Gauls were equally typical in their representation of the inward man.

The old spiritual tranquillity and repose of Pheidian art were no longer in place at Pergamon and Rhodes, where artists had become familiar with great tides of emotion and with the sensations of terror (as in the Laocoon), pain, intoxication and victory. Their art is an art of display, like the Baroque of later times. In Rome, however, perhaps through the influence of artists coming from Greece proper, a reaction arose against the excesses of Rhodian and Alexandrian art (as against "Asian flamboyance" in literature) and there was a desire to return to the sobriety of the older art. From the first century BC, therefore, copies began to be made at Rome of the older Greek works of art, many of which had been found in Italy, Delos and elsewhere.

Greek art exerted a great influence not only at Rome but as far afield as India. Just as in Egypt Greek artists remodeled Sarapis and Isis in a more Hellenic style, so Greek artists were summoned to the Seleucid state and remodelled the statues of the Buddha, whose religious teaching had been adopted by the great Indian ruler Asoka (a. 270-235 BC), as it was later by the Greek king Menander, who extended his possessions in India as far as the Ganges, unattained even by Alexander the Great. According to W. Weber [78] "the image of the Buddha created by Greek artists remains the symbol of the permanent influence of Greek civilization in Asia." Until the Greeks came it had not been possible to create an iconography of the Buddhist religion; consequently, this bold stroke of theirs exercised a profound influence on the art of Asia. Sculptured works of Greco-Buddhist art have been found in the town of Gandhara in the

[78] W. Weber. *Der Siegeszug des Griechentums im Orient. Die Antike.* Vol. I (1925). p. 101. Also A. von Le Coq. *Auf Hellas Spuren in Ostturkestan* 1926, J. Hankin. "Sculptures Grécobuddhiques du Capisa," in *Monuments et Mémoires de Fondation Piot,* Vol. XXVIII (1925-6), p. 35; G. Boroffka, "Grichische Strickereien aus der Mongolei," in *Die Antike* Vol. III (1927), p. 64; R. Grousset. *De la Grece a la Chine,* 1948.

valley of the Indian Kabul and a few years' study of them has shown that the spread of Buddhism to eastern Turkestan and as far as China carried with it there for centuries, and up to the eighth century AD, the influence of Greco-Buddhist art. Every day works of Greco-Buddhist religious art are being discovered in Afghanistan and in eastern Turkestan. As Grousset says, "Wall paintings have been found which one might consider to be Pompeian, if their subject-matter did not clearly refer to the Buddhist religion. Winged angels have also been found which might be thought to relate to Mithraism, to the art of Dura-Europus or to the early Christian church." In Turkestan, and as far afield as Mongolia and China, it seems that Greek influences also began to operate from some other source, probably through artists from southern Russia, since silk textiles have recently been found with embroideries in Greek style.

As will be clear from these brief observations, the scientific achievement of the Greeks in the time of the Diadochi was great, but greatest of all was their influence on Asia and Egypt. But it would be an endless task if we were to try to follow out in detail the whole of the work of civilization which was performed by the Greeks under Alexander's successors.[79]

[79] I will give only one example of another side of Greek cultural and humanizing influence. According to Strabo, Alexander discontinued in Babylon the law and custom by which the old and infirm were thrown to the dogs in the Bactrian cities, where the bones of those who had been devoured made a fearful spectacle. the tex of Strabo (517) is as follows: "Of these people (the inhabitants of Bactria) the followers of Onesicritus give a not very favourable account. Those who are incapable through age or sickness are thrown to dogs who are kept specially for this purpose and are called in the native language "buriers." And outside the walls of the Bactrian capital everything appears clean but the land inside is mostly crammed with human bones. Alexander put down this custom."

CHAPTER IV

THE ROMAN CONQUEST

The Causes of Roman Success

In the struggles for the unification of ancient Latium the policy was already devised which the Romans were later to follow in subduing and unifying, first Italy, and then the world. The Romans were herdsmen and farmers, not traders; unlike the Greeks, they were not fond of movement and change, but were disciplined and conservative. The Roman family was under an iron discipline and even after death (through the sanctity attached to the will) it continued to obey its head. And family discipline was transferred to the government of the state. Apart from this, the Italian peninsula, which was not as deeply indented as the Greek and did not invite emigration by offering countless bays and harbours, favoured the unification of its inhabitants. When to these factors one adds the Senate, a political organ which secured continuity and experience in Roman policy, there were many advantages operating in Rome's favour and against her antagonists. In particular, the policy of finesse ("divide and rule") was developed by the Senate into an inviolable dogma. The Romans easily succeeded in deluding the Greeks and in gaining the alliance of some against others, usually by promises of liberty and autonomy.

The philosophic historian Polybius (I 1, 5) was already expressing his amazement at the immense conquests of Rome in the second century BC: "What man is there so mean or slothful that he would not wish to know how, or under what manner of constitution, practically the whole of the inhabited world has been conquered within not quite fifty-three years and has fallen under the sole domination of Rome?"

In modern times, from Montesquieu [80] onwards, many historians have tried to explain the success of the Roman conquest.

53

Of these various explanations I shall refer only to that recently given by Heinze, [81] which is based on the psychological observations of Spranger regarding individuality. According to Heinze, the early Romans, who overcame the Samnites and the Carthaginians, belonged not to the money-making, contemplative or religious types of men, but to the power-seekers who seek to impose and extend their authority. I do not know whether Spranger's observations on the psychological types of mankind are entirely reliable, but even if they are, the problem still remains how it was that the Romans were so prolific in forceful characters that their people as a whole took on this particular type. My own assumption is that the gradual moulding of the Roman state, with its well-disciplined and conservative people faced with disorganized and scattered opponents, is enough to explain Roman supremacy. Heinze's psychological explanation is of interest, like every psychological contribution to the interpretation of historical events and characters, but it does not suffice to explain to us such a huge complex of events as is constituted by the Roman conquest of Italy alone.

The "Value" of the Roman Conquest

It is questionable how far the "grandeur that was Rome" about which there has been so much discussion, was in fact beneficial to the ancient world, and whether the services of Rome to the cause of law were so great as to justify the enslavement of so many peoples. It is questionable whether in fact the overthrow of Carthage by Rome did, as has been claimed by certain writers, save Greco-Latin civilization or whether the destruction of Jerusalem did save Christianity. Carthage had for centuries made war on the Greeks of the west (Marseilles, Italy and Sicily) but had never destroyed them, as Rome did: and even without the fall of Jerusalem Christianity would have spread beyond the bounds of Palestine to an extent which would have made it impossible for Jewish opposition to harm it.

[80] Montesquieu (1689-1755). *Considérations sur les causes de la grandeur des Romains et de leur décadence*, 1734.

[81] R. Heinze. *Von der Ursache der Grösse Roms*, 1925.

The problem becomes clearer if we examine the cases of conquered Gaul [82] and unconquered Germany. The former lost its language, its vitality and its distinctive original culture, which, it may be added, had never obstructed the beneficient Greek influence of Marseilles. Germany, which never knew subjection to Rome, retained not only its native speech but all its vital strength, which later enabled it to destroy the Roman Empire.

Economic and Administrative Failures

But the Roman conquest was responsible for other disasters, material and economic, besides those moral disasters which subjection brings with it. Rome proved unable to develop the economic potentialities of the subject territories in the way that the Greeks had done everywhere they penetrated. By its economic clumsiness and by the inept rapacity of its tax-gatherers the Roman administration destroyed the flourishing economic condition of Magna Graecia. The sack of Corinth was due to the clumsy economic miscalculations of powerful Romans. The Roman tax-gatherers or "publicans" ruined the production of silphium in Cyrenaica and with it the prosperity of that country. We may leave out of account the maladministration of the Roman officials, who were not paid by the state until Augustus's day but were paid by the provinces, and feared neither Roman law nor the Roman judges when they were denounced by subjects and slaves. Even the best Romans, in consequence, men like Sallust, Cicero and Cassius himself, pillaged the provinces they governed. The type of administrator like Verres, who amassed millions in Sicily, was by no means an exception. Whole populations and cities were sold by generals and governors who felt the pressure of military necessity or economic interest or were simply ignorant of economic law.[83] We have condemned the Greek conquest and expansion in Asia, in spite of all the cultural and economic development it brought with it. But even apart from its first

[82] As Chapot said (Le Monde Romain, 1927, p. 485): "Rome a étranglé le celtisme de Gaule."

[83] See C. Barbagallo - G. Bourgin. Le Déclin d'une Civilisation ou la Fin de la Grece Antique, 1927, pp. 258 ff.

achievement, the ruin of Carthage, the Roman conquest caused economic collapse and upheaval through the arbitrariness of its officials and their lack of skill in economic affairs. From Augustus onward the Empire was for a time to govern the world better than the so-called Republic, but the difference between them can hardly justify the Roman conquest.

The wars of Rome were in a sense economic enterprises. The farmers and herdsmen of early Latium, and subsequently of Italy, reaped enormous gains from a successful war. The booty, the slaves, the returns in property and money were abundant. The poorer and unpropertied soldiers obtained estates and settled on them, since the state protected and compensated in every way the soldiers who won it so much glory and so much wealth.[84] But the number of slaves and the amount of wealth which came to Italy transformed not only the economic but also the social and moral situation. While in the east slavery had almost died out under the Ptolemies and Egypt was cultivated by hired labour, Italy was so flooded with slaves that the free labourers could no longer compete[85] with them. They therefore left the land and went to Rome and other cities or sought positions in the provinces or in the military settlements. Agriculture, however, cannot flourish on a slave basis and Italy did not in fact flourish under slave cultivation. From the time of Augustus the State imported the whole of the abundant corn crop of Egypt into Italy in aid of the cities, whose concentrated mass of refugees from the country received free corn and oil. Egypt as an imperial estate, was bound to export its corn to Italy alone. But this gave rise to yet another evil — the contrast between the country, where men endured so much hardship in tilling the soil, and the towns, where the harvest was idleness and corruption. This contrast was to have fateful consequences, as we shall see, but not even the slave revolt under Spartacus, in the first century BC, taught Rome a lesson. The concentration of the Roman herdsmen

[84] As Plutarch says (Tiberius Gracchus VIII, 1). "Of the land which they took from their neighbours by war, the Romans sold some, but a part they made State land (ager publicus) and distributed among the unpropertied and indigent among their citizens, who paid a small rent to the treasury."

[85] Strabo (668) says: "When the Romans became rich after the overthrow of Carthage and Corinth, they took to employing large numbers of slaves."

and farmers in the cities or their dispersal in the illimitable
provinces of the Roman Empire, where they served and
worked as soldiers, officials, moneylenders middlemen,
transformed the Roman character. It was useless to expect
from such conquerors as these the old Roman virtues of stead-
fastness and courage. Humanity did indeed distinguish those
superior minds who had been formed by Greek philosophy,
but not the lesser Romans who looked with contempt on the
Empire's subjects and sought the most convenient way to fleece
them.

Roman Citizens

The original cause of the decline of Rome was the enslavement of so many peoples, which, as has been said, on the one
hand corrupted the ancient Roman character and on the other
gave rise to the debasement and exploitation of the subject
races.[86]

The gradual concession of the privilege of Roman citizenship
(in 89 BC it was granted to the inhabitants of Italy) separated
the privileged persons (the *cives Romani*) from the rest, who
at every point found themselves in an inferior position —
not to speak of the foreign elements who were regarded as
State bondsmen (*peregrini dediticii*), as for instance the
Egyptians, who were regarded as fit only for exploitation.
Nowhere have slaves endured more than they did under the
Roman Empire. In ancient Greece their treatment was far
more humane, while in the Roman Empire, on the great
estates (*latifundia*), in the mines and in the industrial work-
shops their lot was unbelievably hard[87] as regards food, lodg-
ing and forced labour.

In 212 AD the Emperor Caracalla granted the right of
Roman citizenship (*constitutio Antoniniana*) to all inhabitants of the Roman Empire and thus completed the work of

---

[86] A great many imaginative tales have been written about the prevalence
of corruption in Roman times, to which biographies written on the model
of Suetonius and the exaggerations of the Christians have helped to contribute. A notable book on the subject is that of L. Friedländer. *Darstel-
lungen aus der Sittengeschichte Roms in der Zeit von August bis zum
Ausgang der Antoniner*, 9th ed. by G. Wissowa, Vols. I-IV, (1919-21).

[87] Zielinski - Fichelle. *Histoire de la Civilisation Antique*, 1931, p. 330.

his father Septimius Severus, the African, who felt a dislike for the true-born Romans and in this way humiliated the Senate. The right of citizenship was also bound up with the payment of the inheritance tax of 5%, and this consideration also played its part in Caracalla's policy.[88] By the irony of fate, in that same year (212) there took place the murder of the Praetorian Prefect and great jurist of the Empire Papinian. The grant of Roman citizenship was certainly a great advance from the legal point of view, since it recognized the equality of conqueror and subject, Romans and other races; [89] but in practice it did not much improve the situation.

Even as between Roman citizens a distinction was made between "nobler" and "humbler" [90] (*honestiores, humiliores*) and different penal scales were applied to them. Thus, for example, as witnesses in the law courts or as accused, the "humbler" were subjected to various tortures from which the "nobler" were exempted. Similarly, only the *humiliores* were subjected to forced labour in the mines or to scourging, or were condemned to fight with wild beasts.

Foreigners and Romans

While the conquest of the "world   (οἰκουμένη) and the granting of Roman citizenship, first to the whole of Italy and then to the whole world-empire, meant a distribution of Roman citizens throughout the provinces, conversely it brought many foreigners, slaves and others, to Rome and Italy and produced racial changes in the population, first and foremost, of Rome itself. But just as later in America, the accumulation of so many foreigners had its effect on the character of the early English settlers in North America, so too the same

---

88 L. Hartmann. "Der Untergang der Antiken Welt" (in his *Weltgeschichte,* Vols. I and III), p. 228.

89 From 212 onwards all the subjects of Rome were termed Romans, and so in consequence were the Greeks, who were proud of the title, at least so far as the Christian Greeks were concerned. The name "Hellenes" was thereafter applied only to the pagans and in their disfavour: it became rarely used and was used of Christians only in the last centuries of the Byzantine Empire.

90 Zeilinski-Fichelle. *op. cit.,* pp. 452 & 399.

thing happened at Rome. The Romans of imperial times were no longer true descendants of the ancient Romans and their character was not the same. Little by little there developed that individualism which had been so restricted under the discipline of ancient Rome.[91]

It is a sign of the times that — even if we leave Greek influence partly out of account—there were so many foreign writers who were thoroughly, or merely externally, Latinized. From northern Italy, for example, which contained so many foreign racial elements, there came the great poets Vergil, from Mantua and Catullus, from Verona, and the historian Livy, from Padua, the two Plinies, and others. From Spain came the two Senecas and a number of others already mentioned above. In Christian times Africa produced a number of writers. The greatest jurists of the Roman Empire, Gaius (110-180 AD) from Asia Minor,[92] Papinian, from Emesa, and Ulpian, from Tyre, were perhaps Syrian Greeks. Papinian was put to death by the Praetorians in the reign of Caracalla and Ulpian in the reign of Alexander Severus. Papinian and other jurists, such as Evenius Modestinus, wrote also in Greek. Other Greeks, like the historian Ammianus Marcellinus and the poet Claudian, later wrote in Latin.

Even in the administration foreigners also served as officials. In the time of Claudius many Greeks were serving at court and throughout the Empire, both freedmen and others, such as the all-powerful Narcissus, and later Lucian, Appian and Dio Cassius. From the time of Septimius Severus,[93] when Papinian was chief minister, easterners, and particularly Greeks, occupied yet other posts, both political and military.

Illyrians and Germans

In the army the right of Roman citizenship was bound up with military service. Those who did not acquire this right, such as State bondmen, Egyptians and others, did not serve in the army. It is noteworthy that Marius had already intro-

---

[91] W. Otto. *Kulturgeschichte des Altertums*, 1926, pp. 141 & 144.

[92] Vizoukides. *Gaius and his "Institutions"*, Salonica, 1937, (in Greek).

[93] H. Dessau. *Geschichte der römischen Kaiserzeit*, Vol. II (1926); p. 140.

duced mercenaries and had abolished the ancient Roman military system under which the Romans alone had been simultaneously citizens and soldiers. With the extension of the privilege of Roman citizenship the number of foreigners in the army increased, and from 212 onwards a situation was reached in which foreigners alone were serving in it.

It was through the army that foreigners, though of course Latinized foreigners, even attained the imperial throne. Thus we have first the Spanish emperors — Trajan, Hadrian, Marcus Aurelius — then the Africans, Septimius Severus and his son Caracalla, then Philip the Arab, and from Decius (249 and onwards) that series of Illyrian emperors — Claudius from Dardania, Aurelian from Moesia, Probus from Pannonia, Diocletian from Dalmatia, Galerius from Sardica (Sofia), Constantine from Naissus (Nish), and so on — which caused Mommsen to speak of the Illyrianization (*Illyrisierung*) of the Roman army.[94] After Septimius Severus, but still more after Decius, it may be said that the Roman Empire was governed by foreign emperors and foreign officials.

The Illyrians who ruled Rome by the mass of their soldiery were unable to give the least assistance to their homeland, Illyricum. As unlettered soldiers, they exhausted themselves in the service of Rome without any requital for their own native land, just as in modern times the Albanians served Turkey as generals and higher officials without benefit to Albania.

After the working out of the Illyrian vein came the succession of German emperors, with the difference that these not only served Rome but were served by her. Marius had already in 102 BC found it necessary to defeat the first German invaders of Gaul, the Cimbri and Teutones. From the time of Marcus Aurelius there began a gradual settlement of Germans, Marcomanni and others, within the Empire in return for military service. From the third century AD the pressure of the Alamanni, Franks and Goths began to grow; many of them also entered the Roman service. Thus by degrees, over a space of two centuries huge numbers of Germans entered Italy, Gaul

94 Th. Mommsen. *Römische Geschichte*, Vol. V. (1909), p. 228.

and Spain and settled there. Their dissolution of the Roman
Empire in 476 does not therefore, entirely astonish us.

Racial Transformation of the Romans

A gradual change, then, came over the racial character,
not only of Rome but of the whole western half of the Roman
Empire and it can easily be understood that racial homo-
geneity and "Roman" character ceased to exist. The Empire
was taken over by the army and the civil service, which ever
since the time of Augustus had ceased to be a career of honour
for the private citizen and had become by degrees a salaried
service. As time went on, this service devloped a strict hier-
archy, more particularly under Diocletian.

It is clear that, in a time of such racial confusion it was not
easy to rule so vast an empire as the Roman. There were
many sources of opposition. There was opposition from the
large bodies of foreigners, German and Illyrian: the foreign
emperors hated the Senate and the equestrian order, and gradually degraded them. The continuity of the Senate's policy,
which had been so beneficial in ancient times, now ceased.

Rome's conquests, therefore, and her incessant wars, resulted
in the gradual delivering of the state into the hands of foreigners who had no feeling for Rome.

Economic Decline

This, however, was not the only result of the Roman conquest. The enormous numbers of prisoners and slaves who
were brought to Italy were employed in agriculture and industry, but with slave and serf labour production did not flourish
either in ancient Greece or elsewhere. It is typical that, while
the Ptolemies had cultivated Egypt with free or hired labour
and had thus to some extent abolished slavery, Rome, even
after the creation of her mightiest work, Roman law, worked
through slaves and under Diocletian came to employ serfs
as well. For that reason, while under the Ptolemies Egypt became the wealthiest country in the world, the granary of the
Mediterranean, Rome was forced to import corn and other food-
stuffs into Italy from elsewhere. The slaves did their work
badly, the free labourers left the land for the towns, and the

rich found an opportunity of building up huge estates (*lati-fundia*) which, in this vicious circle, made the situation still worse, since they inflicted still greater hardship on the slaves and the remaining free labour. According to the observation of an ancient historian, the *latifundia* ruled Italy, and today we are forced to regard this huge concentration of property in individual hands as having been in fact one of the main con-tributory causes of Roman decline. The fact that in Africa a few Romans managed to seize practically the entire country from its owners and to exploit it, is surely already a symptom of decline, and it helped, with other causes, towards a more rapid decay. For this very reason the great Roman estates in Africa, with their accompanying human degradation, have inevitably attracted the attention and the indignation of many historians, even those who have regarded as essential Rome's destruction of Semitic Carthage. Rome feared Car-thage because she could not compete with her in the economic field; but having destroyed Carthage, she knew no other way of developing Africa than the terrible creation of large estates on which men became beasts or lifeless chattels, a sort of building material.

Generally speaking, the Romans handled economic problems unskilfully and inefficiently. They had originally been herds-men and farmers and they were not able to make the neces-sary radical adjustment in their way of life even after they had conquered the world.[95] Rome knew nothing like the commercial and maritime development of the medieval Italian cities, Venice and Genoa. In spite of the necessities of war which forced the construction of a battle fleet, the Romans never took to the sea. Later on, after the defeat of the Cartha-ginians, it was the Celts who conducted trade in the west, the Greeks and the Syrians in the east and to some extent in the west as well. In Italy itself slaves and freedmen were traders. The Romans preferred the military enterprises which brought them greater profits, rather than navigation and commerce. Like other conquering peoples later, they derived so much profit and such advantages from war and from the countries

[95] The words *pecunia* (money) and *peculium* (property) derive from *pecus* (cattle).

they occupied that they never took the opportunity of developing commercial enterprises as well.[96]

The Romans were often high-handed and crafty in their proceedings. Thus, for instance, the means they chose in 166 BC to fight the Rhodians and to destroy their trade was to found the free harbour of Delos, the use of which they permitted to the Athenians, whom they favoured. A great slave market sprang up there, disposing of 10,000 slaves a day. In the provinces they forbade the production, now of one article, now of another, in accordance with the interests of Rome, which was unable to stand free competition. Economically, they were formidable only as lenders of money, lending customarily at 50, sometimes even at 100 per cent.

Town and Country

When speaking of the Ptolemies, Seleucids and Attalids, we noticed that all of them, but particularly the Seleucids, granted various economic privileges to the towns, while the country folk were heavily taxed and worked both the royal land and that of private owners. This system was followed by the Romans also and, as we have seen, they too founded and encouraged by the grant of privileges Greek cities in the East.

In the West, however, events took a different course. When the long-suffering countrymen left the country and moved to the towns, the Romans were obliged, first, to feed these accumulations of unemployed and then to amuse them with gladiatorial shows, combats with wild beasts and other spectacles, which coarsened still further the unlettered minds of these wretched masses. Thus, largely though the influence of Christianity, they were compelled to make some provision for feeding these people — which was indeed praiseworthy— but this led to a terrible contrast between country and town. The unemployed in the cities demanded "bread and circuses" (*panem et circenses*) and obtained them at great expense to the State, while the inhabitants of the country were taxed and worked like beasts.[97] The unemployed demanded incessantly an increase in the number of their entertainments,

---

96 V. Parvan, *Die Nationalität der Kaufleute im römischen Kaiserreich,* 1909. On the Greeks of Italy and the Italians (few of them Romans) who practised trade, see J. Hatzfeld, *Les Trafiquants Italiens dans l'Orient Hellénique,* 1919, p. 367 ff.

which in the time of Marcus Aurelius amounted to 135 days a year and later to 175. Most of all, condemned criminals were thrown to the beasts, as were Christians at the time of the persecutions. The feeding of the multitudes of unemployed in the cities was, then, not only a demonstration of the economic inefficiency of the State, but the accompanying combats of beasts and gladiators and pantomimic plays also gave rise to the corruption and barbarization of the masses. It was only by a great effort that Christianity later succeeded in quelling the inhuman passion of the Romans for the spectacles of the circus.

While this process was taking place in the cities, the population of the countryside were suffering the extremes of misery from taxation and forced labour. Many poor farmers were forced to seek the patronage (*patrocinium*) of rich landowners, as in an earlier age the plebeians (*clientes*) had that of patricians.   This patronage, which was retained at Byzantium too for some centuries, gave still greater power to the owners of the large estates who gathered in huge revenues without any benefit accruing from these to the State, disposed of private armies, and often formed a state within the State itself.[98]

In such circumstances it was inevitable that the economic life of Rome should decline, that the enormous wealth amassed through Rome's conquests should be dissipated and that a money economy should sink to one based on barter and exchange. Thus, by the third century AD, Rome had, among her other distresses, arrived at an economic impasse. Neither the succession of great emperors in the second century AD (Trajan, Hadrian, Antoninus Pius, Marcus Aurelius) nor that of the Illyrian commanders of the third century (Aurelian and the rest) could forestall or arrest economic collapse. With their military mentality, the Romans turned for their sovereign remedy to various forms of force and constraint. By degrees government and military service, and professional service as well, was made obligatory. Everything was subjected

97 F. Lot. *La Fin du Monde Antique et le Début du Moyen Age*, 1927, pp. 204, 208. On the provision of food for the unemployed and the poor or large families in the towns see too Ed. Gebhard, *Studien über das Verpflegungswesen von Rom und Constantinopel in der späteren Kaiserzeit*, 1881.

98 Lot. *op. cit.* p. 149 ff.

to military regimentation. The soldier, the civil servant, the skilled workman, the farmer were compelled to serve, and their children with them. Seamen(*navicularii*) were compelled to transport corn and other goods from Africa to Italy, wood-cutters were compelled to cart wood for the army.

The Roman conquests, then, produced national and racial transformation and opposition with, first, economic and social upheaval and then collapse on all fronts. These forced the emperors [99] to pay some attention to religion. Aurelian thought that he could save the empire through the cult of Helios-Mithras, Diocletian by making war on the Christian enemies of the State, Constantine, finally, by making friends with Christianity. But with the victory of Christianity the whole of the ancient Greco-Roman world passed into the Middle Ages.

Opinions on the Decline of Rome

The problem of the decline of Rome and of the ancient world in general is, as Lot has truly said, "the greatest and most important problem of world history." From what has been said above it is clear that we cannot attribute this decline to any one factor: let us, however, on this point quote at least the views of a number of historians to show how difficult the problem is.

Ferrero [100] attributed the decline of Rome to purely political causes, to the emperors' opposition to the Senate from the time of Septimius Severus onward and to the dissolution of senatorial power. The continuity of policy in ancient Rome, which had given the Romans such a superiority in the face of their loosely organized antagonists and had brought such a weight of experience to bear on the country's major problems, ceased to exist. Yet the elements of decay had been present even before Septimius Severus and the safety of the world cannot have depended entirely on the personalities of the

[99] *Op. Cit.* p. 197.

[100] C. Ferrero. *La Ruine de la Civilisation Antique*, 1921, p. 46.

Senate any more than it did on the personalities of the great
emperors of the second and third centuries.

Seeck, [101] in his very important six-volume study of the
"downfall of the ancient world," has, under the influence of
biological theories, attributed this decline to the "eradica-
tion of the fittest" (*Ausrottung der Besten*) owing to the endless wars. Geyer, under the influence of Nazism, attributed
the decline of the Roman Empire to the diminution of Nordic
blood (Rass, *Volk und Staat im Altertum*, 1936. p. 172).

Many historians, L. Hartmann and others, accept the old
theory, according to which the great estates, the unequal distribution of property and its consequences, and the economic
problems to which these gave rise, produced first an impasse
and then decay. This theory was opposed by Rostovezeff,[102]
who, while drawing attention to the economic wealth of many
of the provinces and cities of the Roman Empire, noted a
fatal contrast betwen the workless, unconscripted populations
of the towns and the soldiery drawn from the country. These
barbarian soldiery (more particularly from 212 AD onwards)
produced a sort of mental barbarization of the Roman
Empire.

Rostovtzeff, however, as also Hohl, [103] remarks that it is
impossible to account by simple explanations for so huge and
complex an event as the decline of the ancient world. Its causes
were multiple and according to Hohl we should speak rather
of the transition from the ancient to the medieval world than
of the collapse of the former.

My own belief is that the subjugation of so many peoples
is the easiest explanation both of the economic maldistribution
and unrest and also of the moral corruption to which these
gave rise. In so far as the Greeks underwent the religious
influence of the East, as has been said above, an influence to
which the Romans were in no position to provide a counter-

[101] O. Seeck. *Geschichte des Unterganges des Antiken Welt*. Vol. I
(1897), p. 270.

[102] *The Social and Economic History of the Ancient World*, 1926, p. 482:
"The economic explanation of the decay of the Ancient World must be
rejected completely."

[103] E. Hohl "Die Römische Kaiserzeit," *Propyläen-Weltgeschichte*, Vol.
II (1931), p. 467.

weight, it can easily be understood how the ancient world came to lie at the mercy of religion. The Roman conquest and enslavement brought on economic and moral collapse and, in consequence, forced mankind to seek refuge in the Christian Middle Ages.

CHAPTER V

GREECE AND ROME

Influence of Greek Civilization on the Romans

The Greeks established few settlements on the Illyrian coast (Epidammus-Dyrrachium), but later the tyrant Dionysius founded settlements from Sicily on the islands of Corfu, Issa (Hvis), Pharos (Hvar) and elsewhere. They found it a good deal easier to settle in the more fertile parts of Sicily and southern Italy, as far north as Campania, where the most northerly Greek city in Italy, Cumae, was founded. Greek culture thus spread rapidly and even produced philosophers like Zeno the Eleatic and Pharmenides, and in Sicily Empedocles of Agrigentum; it also exercised a civilizing effect on the various other native races of Italy. The economic and cultural activities of the Greeks made their presence welcome. The Romans first received the Greek alphabet from Cumae; later they also came under the influence of Greek religion and almost the whole of the Roman pantheon was modelled on Greek originals. The names of many deities were changed and became Greek names and the Greek mythology relating to these gods was taken over. The Romans likewise received the books of the Sibyl of the temple of Apollo at Cumae. The Greeks of Italy also influenced the coinage of the Romans, Tyrrhenians and Etruscans: even the creators of Roman law who later became so famous were influenced in the fifth century BC by the legislation of Zaleucus of Locri and Harondas of Catania.[104]

The benefits which the Italian Greeks conferred on the

---

[104] Em. Ciaceri. *Storia della Magna Grecia*, Vols. I & II 2nd ed., 1927; M. Homs. *La Civilisation Ramaine* 1938. p. 82 ff., 216 ff; J. Bérard. *La Colonisation Greque de l'Italie méridionale et de la Sicile dans l'Antiquité. L'Historie et la Légende*, Paris 1941; T. Dunbabin. *The Western Greeks* 1948.

Romans, in particular, were repaid with destruction. There is no more tragic history than that of the Greeks of Italy and Sicily who were obliged to struggle against the Italians and the Carthaginians, and to some extent against the Etruscans as well, and never succeeded in uniting.

First, the city of Cumae made war with the Latins in 500 BC against the Etruscans. In 474 the Tyrrhenian fleet was defeated by Hiero, I, tyrant of Syracuse, who also defeated the Carthaginians off Himera in Sicily. Unluckily, Hiero failed to unite the Greeks in a single powerful state. An excessive love of independence wrecked, even in Sicily, the attempts made to weld together a larger Greek commonwealth. In consequence the Carthaginians were able, between 409 and 406 BC, to overcome the cities of Selinus, Himera and Acragas and to occupy the southern side of the island.

Dionysius (405-467 BC), who was a man of strong character, succeeded in acquiring two thirds of Sicily and the southern regions of. Italy and thereby forming a powerful state, but his failings helped to bring about his overthrow. It is worth noting, however, that he despatched settlements to the Dalmatian islands in order to buttress himself against his enemies from the north. As E. Meyer [105] says, "if the state created by Dionysius had been maintained, the development of world history would have been different." The most important Greek city of southern Italy was Tarentum (Taras), which had been at pains to secure the famous Heracles of the sculptor Lysippus. The Aristotelian philosopher and musician, Aristoxenus was a Tarentine. The city waged a series of conflicts with the southern Italian peoples, the Messapii, the Iapyges, the Samnites, the Lucanians and the Bruttii, and repeatedly sought to this end the help of experienced generals from Greece, Archidamus the son of Agesilaus, Alexander the Molossian from Epirus, and Cleonymus the son of Cleomenes (301). Archidamus fought gallantly and was killed in 338, Alexander in 331. Later on, the Romans in their turn took up the struggle against Tarentum and the other Greek cities, and Pyrrhus, King of Epirus,[106] who was summoned to Italy, failed in the end to defeat them. Tarentum was taken in 272 BC. Thenceforward

105 E. Meyer. *Klein Schriften*, I, p. 243.

106 Ciaceri. *Storia della Magna Graecia*, Vol. III (1932), pp. 6 ff., 25 ff.

Magna Graecia was subject to the Romans but it was from conquered Tarentum that the art of letters came to Rome through Livius Andronicus.

In Sicily a competent military leader made his appearance, namely Hiero II, tyrant of Syracuse, who began by defeating the Mamertines at Messina (265-4). Although he also fought bravely against the Carthaginians, he was forced to conclude a treaty with the Romans, who having secured the victory, proceeded to destroy Akragas (Agrigentum), which Berve [107] has called "one of the most brilliant of the Greek cities."

The war which the Greeks of Magna Graecia had thus to wage on two fronts, against the Romans and against the Carthaginians, and the failure of their attempts to unite under a single ruler in the end brought about their downfall.

Literature

Among the Greeks taken prisoner at Tarentum was Andronicus, who became tutor at Rome to the children of a certain Livius, whose name is added to his own. In 240 Andronicus translated the Odyssey into Latin verse, in the Saturnian metre, for the benefit of his pupils, and he later composed both tragedies and comedies after Greek models. The example of Livius Andronicus was soon followed by other poets, Naevius (264-194 BC), Ennius (239-169 BC) and Plautus, all of whom came from the outlying parts of Italy (Campania, Apulia and elsewhere), where Greek was known. These writers translated or arranged plays of the New Comedy or wrote original compositions (Ennius even employed the heroic hexameter) on historical events in their own country. The earliest Latin poetry, therefore, was borrowed and imitative and gave rise to a certain friendly feeling for Greece, as is shown by the relatively liberal political utterances of Flamininus in Greece (194 BC).

Latin prose literature began in the second century BC and it is typical that the first writers, such as Fabius Pietor, wrote in Greek. This, however, provoked a reaction on the part of the conservative-minded Romans, who feared foreign influences in other directions also, and the severe Cato ven-

[107] H. Berve. *Griechische Geschichte*, Vol. II (1933), p. 201.

tured to write his own historical treatise in Latin, without
however escaping the influence of the Greek historians. By
his example Cato not only laid the foundations of Latin
prose but taught the general lesson that independent creation
is always a finer thing than blind imitation. His example was
not unique. The reaction against Greek influence was widespread
and showed itself also in the inhuman policy of Aemilius
Paullus in Greece after 168 BC. The Romans feared Greek
culture as a solvent of their own stern moral code and it
was on this account that in 193 BC they expelled the Greek
Epicurean philosophers as particularly dangerous.

Fine Arts

Greek influence could not, even so, be halted by this opposition. Greek sculpture, painting and architecture could not
fail to be imitated at Rome. Already in the fifth century BC
the first temple of Ceres-Demeter at Rome was decorated by
the Greek painters Damophilus and Gorgasus. Similarly, even
the symbol of Rome itself, the first bronze she-wolf set up in
the Capitol, seems to have been the work of Greek artificers;
and even at the height of the reaction Cato himself founded,
in 184 BC, the first Roman basilica, the *Basilica Porcia,* on
the model of a similar building at Pompeii. From that time
the type of the Hellenic basilica became widely distributed.
The same process took place with the Hellenic porticoes, one
of which, the Stoa of Metellus, was built by the Cypriot
architect Hermodorus, who also erected temples of Demeter
and Hera in the second century BC. These temples were
adorned with statues by the sculptor Timarchides. Roman
generals returning from Greece brought with them large
numbers of statues which aroused interest in the capital, and
after their rediscovery in modern times adorn countless
Italian museums today. The Greeks of Magna Graecia, too,
produced great craftsmen like Pasiteles and Arcesilaus. Pasiteles established a school at Rome and wrote on the sculptural
works of Greek antiquity. As time went on, Greek artists were
called in to copy the works of the great masters for the villas
of cultured Romans or to paint the villas themselves. As a
result, the art of cities like Pompeii and Herculaneum, and of

Rome itself, was in large part Greek. Even Augustus, with his conservative mind and his reverence for ancestral custom, was obliged to model his palace on the Palatine hill after Greek originals, and his friend Agrippa did likewise with the baths which he built. Later, Septimius Severus was to build the huge Septizonium in the manner of the Hellenistic *Nymphaea* of Asia Minor and Aurelian was to imitate Greek military architecture in constructing the new walls of Rome. Augustus, again, despite his conservatism, was forced to have recourse to the Greek artist Dioscurides for the engraving of his signet ring.

The growing interest in art, the importation of Greek vases and the copying of works of sculpture reached such a pitch that artistic currents began to form in Rome itself, sometimes archaistic, sometimes modern in style. In the time of Augustus, for instance, the prevailing tendency was to copy ancient works. But the great urban centres of Greek civilization in the east, the great temples and palaces, set new architectural problems, especially in Syria and in regions where there was a dearth of timber. It was thus that the stone dome and the stone arch came into being, both being later adopted at Rome, where the curved lines of the east had already been introduced in earlier times by Etruscan civilization. A Greek architect, Apollodorus, built the Roman Pantheon in the second century AD and was the first to introduce the hemispherical dome on a circular drum. The same architect executed a number of works in Rome on the orders of Hadrian. Earlier on, in Trajan's time, Apollodorus had built the Forum and Column of Trajan, together with the bridge over the Danube by the modern Turnu Severin.[108]

Philosophy

The period from Aemilius Paullus to Pompey covers the unhappy time of the subjection and humiliation of Greece. The conquering Romans haled thousands of Greeks into captivity, often by a process of deliberate selection, as in the case

---

108 On the influence of Greek art see too A. Grenier. *Le Génie Romain dans la Religion, la Pensée et l'Art*, 1925, p. 279 ff; H. Tsountas. *History of Ancient Greek Art.* 1928, p. 520 ff. (in Greek).

of the enslavement of Polybius. They plundered the art and the wealth of the country, ruined the economy of Macedonia and other provinces by prohibiting the working of metal and other sources of livelihood, thrust the population of the East into Western Asia (in 88 BC, through the agency of Mithridates) and drove much of the population to take to piracy. According to Kahrstedt, this was the age which gave rise to the socialism and communism of the ancient world.[109]

Yet it was during this worst period of all, the period of the downfall and the exploitation of Greece and the East at the hands of the Romans, that Greek philosophy, like Greek art, came to Rome and induced some degree of humanity. Aemillius Paullus himself brought with him the painter Metrodorus. Tiberius Gracchus seems to have been influenced by the Stoic Blossius, his friend, and by Diophanes.[110] The Stoic Panaetius of Rhodes and later his disciple Posidonius (144-60 AD) came and taught at Rome, where their teaching found an echo and nobly inspired many of the great representatives of the Roman spirit—Cicero, who was the first to publicize at Rome the teachings of the Stoics, Seneca at a later date, and finally the man who was perhaps the noblest Roman of them all, the Emperor Marcus Aurelius. The humanizing influence of the Stoic philosophy appears clearly in the famous letter of the philosopher Seneca (No. 47) which deals with the necessity for a more humane treatment of slaves. Marcus Aurelius certainly knew the work of yet another noble Stoic, the slave Epictetus from Hierapolis in Phrygia, whose dissertations had been written down by Arrian. It has been thought that the expulsion of Epictetus from Rome by Domitian in 89 or 92 AD deeply moved Marcus Aurelius and contributed further to his enlightenment. The philosophy of the Stoics formed the Roman *humanitas* (which was also the humane teaching of Isocrates) and had

109 U. Kahrstedt. "Das Zeitalter des antiken Sozialismus and Kommunismus,", in *Hellas-Jahrbuch*, 1929, p. 105 ff.

110 Plutarch. *Tiberius Gracchus*. VIII, 6: " . . . at the instigation of the rhetor Diaphanes and the philosopher Blossius, Diophanes being an exile from Mytilene and Blossius a Cumaean from Italy itself." For the influence of Greek philosophy on the Gracchi, see the *Cambridge Ancient History*, Vol. IX (1932), pp. 21 and 869.

its effect on Roman law, and through Roman law on the whole world.

It was not only philosophers who came to Rome; there were also many other homeless and refugee Greeks or half-Greeks, especially from Syria (the Syrian Greeks were in a sense the "Levantines" of the ancient world), who most probably gave rise to the type of the *Graeculus*. [111] This kind of 'Greekling' was held in contempt but this could not prevent the spread of Greek influence or the extension of the Greek language even to Rome itself, which caused Juvenal to say later, "I cannot endure a Greek Rome."[112] Large numbers of Greeks came to Rome — teachers, doctors, traders, soldiers, prisoners of war and others — so that the Greek language was heard everywhere. Juvenal's indignation was thus justified.

So great was the influence of philosophy, and with it of rhetoric, that they actually came to form the ordinary curriculum and the standard ideal of the Romans, who frequented schools and teachers in Greece in quest of education. Thus, Cicero visited the Levant, as did Brutus, Cassius, Caesar and many others. Given such a degree of influence as this, one can understand Horace's dictum, that captive Greece overcame her fierce conqueror. (*Graecia capta ferum victorem cepit.*) But the use of the Greek language and the literary movement were so strong in Rome that the doctrines of the "Atticizers" were imposed there, a development which according to Jüthner "decided for centuries the fate of Greek letters."

To sum up, the culture of Rome may be considered a Greek culture. The Romans owed to Greece their literature, their philosophy, their art, science, learning, rhetoric and mythology. It was Greece who humanized Rome.[113]

Roman Philhellenes

The subjugation of Greece by the Romans brought terrible disasters in its train, both human and economic. The subjugation of Macedonia and the defeat of Philip V (196 BC) and Perseus (167 BC), followed by the capture of Corinth (146 BC),

[111] J. Jüthner. *Hellenen und Barbaren*, 1923, p. 63.

[112] *Non possum ferre Graecam Urbem.*

[113] M. Croiset. *La civilisation de la Grece Antique*, 1943, p. 332.

caused economic collapse and desolation, especially in Epirus, where the towns were destroyed by Aemilius Paullus and the population was enslaved. The support of the oligarchic or plutocratic factions by the Romans brought ruin to the poorer Greeks: it is for this reason that in the massacre of the Romans in 88 BC by Mithridates we find the rich adherents of the conquerors also the objects of attack. As Kahrstedt says in his interesting study,[114] "The mere presence of Roman officials was often enough to cause spoliation." Again, according to the same scholar, "The 'liberation' of a country by the Romans meant economic disaster and the captivity of its population." Men who had formerly been prosperous were obliged to sell even their children to the Roman moneylenders.[115] In desperation the people took to the mountains and became robbers or went over to Mithridates and Tigranes, the enemies of the Romans. The second century BC gave birth to socialism and communism, "as a protest against Roman rapacity and injustice."[116] Later the civil wars which were waged in Greece by the Romans from 86 BC (when Sulla defeated the army of Mithridates at Chaeronea) to 31 BC, caused such distress and devastation as could not be repaired again in classical times.

It may be said, however, that the Romans in high authority, recognizing the permanent value of Greece, tried to make good these disasters. Thus, for instance, Caesar rebuilt Corinth in 44 BC after its sack by the Romans following the taking of the city in 146. Above all, the emperors from Augustus onwards tried to heal the wounds of Greece by the bestowal of autonomy, by various benefactions to Greek cities, by the founding of temples and by the grant of citizenship. Certain emperors such as Hadrian and Marcus Aurelius showed particular kindness to Greece. This shows how great the influence of Greek culture was and how receptive to culture the Romans were. In fact, Greek culture gave a higher moral tone to the Roman Empire, which was thus enabled to frame Roman law, the greatest of its achievements.

Rome imposed the Latin language on the Italian, Celtic,

114 *Hellas-Jahrbuch*, 1929, p. 108.

115 *Hellas-Jahrbuch*, 1929, p. 114.

116 *Ibid.*, p. 118.

Iberian and even Dacian peoples, but never so much as thought of Latinizing the Greek East. On the contrary, Rome always assisted the spread of Greek in the belief that it was thus advancing the culture and the civilization of the Orient.

The friendly attitude of many emperors and other highly placed Romans — there was no question of the lower officials — was recognized by the Greeks, who often showed their gratitude in a somewhat fulsome manner. To take only one characteristic passage from the speech by the rhetor Aelius Aristides [117] "On Rome": "You care for the Greeks continually like nurselings, stretching out your hands over us and, as it were, raising up them that are fallen . . . leaving the best of us in freedom and independence and those who have from of old been our leaders, treating the rest mildly and with great forbearance and consideration, and educating the barbarians according to the particular nature of each."

The Roman upper classes both in Republican and in Imperial times sought eagerly "to become thoroughly Hellenized, at least in mind, to absorb Greek ethics, education, art and science," [118] to defend Greek civilization everywhere in the East. But this "tragic" policy, as Mommsen calls it, was not destined to save Rome. The enslavement of peoples is the greatest of human crimes and demands expiation. Barbarian conquerors have always been directly punished, often by complete extermination. The Greeks themselves, the most beneficent and civilized of conquerors, paid the penalty by their dispersion. After the Greeks the Romans, despite their efforts to follow in the footsteps of Greek civilization, were gradually corrupted as a result of the enslavement of the ancient world,[119] and fell into decline.

The significant point is that when the Greeks succumbed to the religious influence of the East, they dragged the Romans after them, since the latter had nothing to oppose to the oriental mysteries and magic except the worship of the Emperor as the embodiment of the State. But neither the forcible imposition

[117] Keil's edition, Vol. II (1898), pp. 96, 119.

[118] Th. Mommsen. *Römische Geschichte*, Vol. V, 6th ed. (1909), p. 23.

[119] See the observations of D. de Sanctis in "Der Hellenismus und Rom," *Propyläen-Weltgeschichte*, Vol. II, (1931), p. 323.

of this worship nor the persecution of the Christians could stay the influence of the East, and later of Christianity. The most efficient of the emperors, Constantine the Great, set the example of submission to the new eastern religion, Christianity, and the Romans followed the majority of the Greeks in this respect.

Christianity and the Latin Language

The first Christian writers wrote in Greek, even in Rome itself, where the Popes themselves in the first centuries were frequently Greeks. In addition to St. Paul, Bishops Clement and Hermas wrote in Greek at Rome, while Polycarp of Smyrna likewise taught there in Greek in 154. In Gaul too Christianity was at first preached in Greek.[120] In the course of the third century AD the needs of evangelization led to the use of Latin as well, a step which helped to complete the Latinization of the Latin-speaking countries, where no other language was required. In the East Christianity employed, in addition to Greek, the Aramaic, Coptic and Armenian languages, and later Arabic and Slavonic as well, thus giving rise to native literatures in each of these tongues. In the West, however, after the first translations had been made from the Greek, Latin alone was used in the churches of all the peoples concerned. It was perhaps owing to the use of Latin, which was not understood by the natives, that Christianity disappeared from northern Africa after the Arab conquest, while the use of Coptic helped to save the Christians of Egypt.

Latin theology is found in a dependent relation to Greek in the third and even in the fourth century, when even the theological works of St. Ambrose (d. 397) cannot be understood apart from his eastern predecessors, Basil the Great first and foremost, but also Gregory Nazianzene and Eusebius. The Gallic bishop of Poitiers, Hilary, was the first to borrow ecclesiastical hymns from the East, at the time when he was an exile in Phrygia.

Jerome, from Dalmatia (335-420), was probably of Greek

120 P. Wendland in Grecke-Norden's, *Einleitung in de Alterumswissenschaft,* Vol. I (1922), p. 398.

origin:[121] he spent some time at Constantinople and in Syria
and made a translation of the Bible (the version called the
Vulgate, as constituting the "popular edition"), as well as
translating or editing works by Origen, Eusebius and other
eastern scholars. Other translations were made by Rufinus of
Aquileia (d. 410) and other writers. The appearance of outstanding Latin theologians in Africa is also attributable to
the Greek education which had been widely available there
ever since the time of Hadrian. Africa followed Asia Minor in
its long line of churchmen. Tertullian (d. 230) of Carthage
had received a Greek education and on becoming a Christian
he discarded his Roman habit and dressed as a sophist.
Cyprian also, Bishop of Carthage and martyr (d. 258) and
Lactantius (d. 325), the "Christian Cicero," who taught in
Latin at Nicomedia, bear witness to Greek influence.

In the west, however, a severance of contact with the Greek
tongue had already in the fifth century produced an intellectual
decline, immediately after the time of Augustine (354-430),
who by his theocratic work on the City of God (*De Civitate
Dei*) paved the way, as it were, directly to the Dark Ages.
The Greek Claudian and the Gaul Ausonius, both of whom
wrote in Latin, were exceptions, but they cannot be said to
alter the general situation.

From Bordeaux, where some knowledge of Greek survived,
it reached Ireland where it was preserved and became more
influential than on the mainland of Europe.[122]

For a brief moment letters once again exercised some
influence in Italy when, after the settlement of the Ostrogoths
under Theodoric and after the Gothic wars of Justinian, communication was once more resumed with the East. The last
writer to come under the spell of Greece was Boethius who
in 523-4 wrote his *Consolatio Philosophiae* in prison; but
after that date Greek had no futher influence.

The Conquest of Greece by the Romans

It has been said above that the reduction in the population

---

[121] E. Norden. "Die lateinische Literatur im Ubergange vom Altertum
zum Mittelalter," in Hinneberg's *Die Kultur der Gegenwart*, I, VIII,
(1905), p. 380.

[122] W. Moellendorff. *Geschichte der Philologie*, 1921, p. 6.

of Greece facilitated the Roman conquest: there were, however, other highly important contributory factors. While the
Roman Senate had been following a steady and continuous
policy and had kept the people and the army under strict
discipline, in Greece and the East wars had ensued between
the Diadochi and the new states of the Achaean and Aetolian
federations, and in the face of the united Romans the Greeks
were not only disorganized and at variance but even fought in
alliance with the Romans against each other. It can thus be
said, not that Rome conquered Greece but that Greece was
occupied by Rome. The Roman Senate had only to apply
its policy of intrigue, as Eduard Meyer says[123] to bring
distracted Greece under control.

There were men in Greece, like Agelaus of Naupactus, who
recognized the Roman peril in the days of Philip V of
Macedon and pleaded for concord [124] and for the abandonment
of civil war, but their voices could not be heard.[125] The geographical factors which had assisted the emigration and the
thinning of the population and the disbandment of cities and

---

[123] E. Meyer. *Blüte und Niedergang des Hellenismus in Asien*, 1926, p. 62.

[124] Plutarch regarded a united Greece as invincible: "But, most of all,
they (the Achaeans) showed that the strength of Greece was unbeatable
whenever there was order and harmonious organization and intelligent
leadership," (*Aratus*, IX. 5). The historian Zosimus (A. III, 1) was also
of the opinion that a united Greece would be invincible: "If the Athenians
and the Spartans had not fallen out in their rivalry with each other over
the leadership of the Greeks, others would never have become the masters
of Greece."

[125] According to Polybius (V. 104), Agelaus recommended that "the Greeks
ought never make war on each other but . . . should join hands, like men
crossing a river, and in concert save themselves and their cities . . . He
considered that all should watch for the right moment to act, but particularly Philip. His best security would be to leave off destroying the
Greeks and making them an easy prey to invaders and rather to take
counsel for them as for his own person and to make provision generally,
for every part of Greece as if it were his own possession. And if he longs
for action he had better cast his eyes on the west and pay attention to
the wars in progress in Italy . . ." Agelaus speaks prophetically of
"clouds appearing from the west." Other soldiers and statesmen, like
Pyrrhus and Demetrius of Pharos, foresaw the Roman danger, but no one
was able to prevent civil conflict and unite even the Greeks of Italy and
Sicily. It is typical of Greek dissensions that Ptolemy II congratulated
the Romans after the defeat of Pyrrhus and the fall of Tarentum in
272 BC.

which had hindered the unification of the Greeks, now caused
their subjugation by the Romans who up to that time had not
been given to emigration and were united and well disciplined.
The geographical contrast bètween Greece and Italy helped to
bring about the subjection of one to the other.

At first the subjugation of Greece brought in its train
great human and economic calamities. Aemilius Paullus carried off thousands of the inhabitants of Macedonia and Epirus.
Corinth was destroyed, just as Akragas in Sicily had been
earlier on, when the Romans seized that island. The officials
who came to Greece and the East, apart from a few Philhellenes
among the more highly placed Romans, had all the harshness
and insensibility of the conqueror, as well as the taste for
plunder.[126]

Latin and Greek — the Language Problem

Gradually, Rome evolved a special policy towards the
Greeks. First of all, no attempt was made to impose the Latin
language on them; consequently, Latin was not known in the
East except by the Greek officials and soldiers of Rome. The
Illyrians, the Thracians, the inhabitants of Dacia (the modern
Roumania) were Latinized to a certain extent (their modern
descendants the Albanians have in part, and the Aromuni or
Koutzo-Vlachs have to a much greater degree, preserved their
Latin culture) but not the Greeks. Only a few Iberian tribes
(the modern Basques),[127] who had fled into the inaccessible
mountains of northern Spain, kept their own language. Yet
in Spain, too, the policy of Latinization was pursued through
conscription, through the establishment of military settlements
(the name of the modern province of Leon comes from the
Latin *legio*), through the administration which ignored the
use of any other language, and through the privileges and
favours bestowed on those who entered the Roman Army and
on Roman citizens. The Latinization of Spain was so thorough
that some of the greatest emperors came from that country
(Trajan, Hadrian, Marcus Aurelius, Theodosius), besides

[126] H. Dessau. *Geschichte der römischen Kaiserzeit*, Vol. II, 2, (1930), p.
535 ff.

[127] V. Chapot. *Le Monde Romain*, 1927, p. 192.

scholars and poets (the two Senecas, Lucan from Cardova, the geographer Pomponius Mela, Quintilian, Martial, Sallust and others). All these were Latinized Spaniards or Romans from the settlements in Spain. The fact that the Church employed Latin undoubtedly contributed later to the more complete Latinization of the country. Prudentius, who was perhaps the greatest poet of the Latin Church, was a Spaniard,

In the East, the Romans not only did not impose Latin, but actually assisted the spread of Greek, which brought Greek civilization in its train and reduced the barbarity of the natives. The strengthening of Greek culture was regarded by the Romans as being not only in the interest of the State but also beneficial to their subjects.

Egypt under the Romans

A few observations may be added about the other provinces. In Egypt the Romans followed the policy laid down by the Ptolemies, but applied it more harshly. They made absolutely no attempt to Latinize the Egyptians, whom in any case they despised: indeed in 212 Roman citizenship was bestowed by Caracalla on all the subjects of Rome excepting only the Egyptians, the latter being regarded as prisoners of war (*dediticii*). Only the highest officials, military and financial, were Romans, whose responsibility it was to gather in the huge revenues of the Egyptian temples and to supervise the worship of the Emperor, who in Egypt was deified even in his lifetime, Augustus as Jupiter, Caligula as Helios and others as other gods, according to each individual case.[128] The rest of the officials were Greeks. Greek was the language used in the law courts and Greeks were admitted to the Roman legions, but not Egyptians, lest these should at any time become dangerous. The Romans exploited the Egyptians even more than the Greeks had done and had no use for them except as cultivators of the corn which they needed for Italy (its export elsewhere was forbidden) and as taxpayers. Unlike the Ptolemies, the Romans founded no cities in Egypt, obviously in order not to change the agrarian character of the country which served them so well. The only exception was Hadrian's

128 J. Vogt. *Römische Politik in Aegypten*, 1924, p. 14 ff.

foundation of Antinoopolis in memory of his favourite,
Antinous, where intermarriage was permitted with Egyptians
though prohibited elsewhere.

Syria and Mesopotamia

We have said in another place that, by contrast with the
Ptolemies, the Seleucids founded a large number of cities
in Syria and Mesopotamia. Under Parthian rule too, Greek
civilization was to some extent preserved, since the Parthians
did not oppose it; indeed, the Arsacid rulers wished to be
termed, and to be, "Philhellene" and even presented at their
court the works of Greek tragedians (the *Bacchae* of
Euripides). But the famous city of Seleucia on the Tigris
was destroyed in 164 AD when the Parthians defeated the
Romans. Thenceforward, its suburb Ctesiphon rose to prosperity
under the Arsacids, and subsequently under the Sassanids, until
the coming of the Arabs who founded Baghdad (762 AD).
Besides Seleucia, the city of Europus (Dura) was a notable
centre of Greek culture in Mesopotamia, as recent excavations
have strikingly shown.

In Syria the Romans founded the city of Berytus (Beirut),
where a famous school of law flourished later under celebrated
Greek and Hellenized teachers. Hadrian founded on the site of
the ruins of Jerusalem the colony of Aelia Capitolina in which
Roman soldiers were forbidden to live. These Roman cities in
no way hindered the spread of Greek culture in Syria, where
Greek and Syrians drew more and more closely together and
the latter came more and more under Greek influence. In the
country districts, however, the Aramaic language prevailed,
as has already been noted.

Particular emphasis must be laid on the protection which
the Greek language enjoyed in the Arab territories, in the
country of the Nabataeans and its capital, Petra. According to
Mommsen,[129] ". . . while no Greek monument is to be found
from any date prior to Trajan, no Aramaic monument has
been found later than the reign of Trajan. It seems that as
soon as the Romans penetrated there, they discouraged the use
of Aramaic." A number of Greek inscriptions have been found

[129] Mommsen. *Römische Geschichte*, Vol. V (1909), p. 402.

in the Arab country of the Nabataeans, only because the Romans
protected the Greek language there. Greek culture spread even
to Petra, the capital of *Palestina Tertia*.[130]

Under Roman rule Greek cultural influence was greatly
strengthened to the east and south of the Hauran (Auranitis)
where the ruins of Bostra and a number of other cities are to
be found to this day. It was in this region that, according to
Mommsen, the use of the stone arch and the stone dome was
developed owing to the lack of timber.[131] Similarly, the community of the Decapolis was established beyond Jordan, with
the cities of Philadelphia, Heliopolis, Damascus and others.
Even in Arab Palmyra, with its autonomous administration
under *decemvirs* (δεκαπρῶτοι), Greek was spoken in the upper
classes of society up to the time of its destruction by Aurelian
(273 AD). It was in Palmyra that that famous scholar, the
Neoplatonist Longinus,[132] worked and there that he met his
death in the sack of the city.

Asia Minor

As noted elsewhere, Greek civilization found no difficulty
in making progress in the cities of Asia Minor, both because
their inhabitants were in contact with the Greeks of the sea-
board and because the natives were not in a position to oppose
to it any civilization or political organization of their own.
Its progress in Cappadocia and Pontus was harder and slower,
for which reason the Romans founded cities in those regions,
with the express object of reinforcing Greek influence. In
Cappadocia they founded Caesarea and Tyana and in Pontus
Sebastea and Neocaesarea,[133] This reinforcement of Greek influence in Pontus was chiefly begun by Pompey who after his
victory over Pharnaces, the son of Mithridates, divided the

---

[130] A. Alt. *Die Griechischen Inschriften der Palaestina Tertia*, 1921.

[131] Mommsen. *op cit,*. p.181.

[132] The celebrated book "On the Sublime (περὶ ὕψους) which has been
attributed to Longinus is now thought more likely to be the work of
Dionysius of Halicarnassus. See the Hungarian periodical *Archivum Philo-
logicum*, Vol. LIX (1935), p. 376.

[133] Mommsen. *op. cit.*, p. 305.

country into eleven large districts to which he gave municipal
rights.

The Balkan Peninsula

In the Balkan peninsula Rome supported the influence of
the northern Greeks and carried out the task which should
have been discharged by the Antigonidae of Macedon, since the
Greek kingdom of Lysimachus, which had extended as far as
the Danube, did not survive its founder (d. 281 BC). The
Romans also assisted the Greeks of the Crimea and other parts
of southern Russia against the Scythians, since the Hellenarchs
(that is, the Greek magistrates, as opposed to those of the
non-Greeks [134]) had not the strength to repel b a r b a r i a n
incursions.

On the coast of Moesia (the modern Bulgaria) there were
Greek cities of ancient foundation which were now formed
into a federation by the Romans to make a more effective
defense against the attacks of the Sarmatians and the Getae.
The cities of Tomis or Tomi, Odessus, Callatis, Dionysopolis [135]
and Istrus made up the Confederation of the Pentapolis, and
subsequently, after the addition of Trajan's foundation of
Marcianopolis, the Confederation of the Hexapolis. Even in
the interior of what is now Bulgaria and in Thrace Trajan
reinforced Greek influence by granting municipal rights to
regional groups who thus became privileged associations and
began to thrive. The most important of these cities were
Nicopolis on the Nestus, Plotinopolis on the Hebrus (Maritsa)
(founded by Trajan in honour of his wife Plotina), Sardica
(the modern Sofia), Nicopolis on the Danube (the modern
Nikopol on the river Yantra), Trajanopolis on the Hebrus,
and Hadrianopolis (Adrianople) later founded by Hadrian.
These cities were simultaneously centres of civilization and
of Hellenization and they gathered a large population.
Philippopolis (the modern Plovdiv) is said to have had about
100,000 inhabitants when it was destroyed by the Goths in
251 AD. By contrast with the towns, the country districts
were divided into military zones (στρατηγίαι), which did not

[134] Mommsen. *op. cit.*, p. 305.

[135] O. Tafrali. *La Cité Pontique de Dionysopolis*, 1927.

of course enjoy the privileges of the towns and were governed
by "generals" (στρατηγοί), that is to say by military adminis-
trators.[136]

In Macedonia the Romans did not allow the towns so
many privileges, perhaps because they did not consider it
necessary. So far as the interior of Macedonia is concerned,
it is of little significance that Thessalonike (Salonica) was
granted freedom and self-government by the Romans or that
the Macedonian cities placed the head of Alexander the Great
on their coinage instead of that of the Roman Emperor.

In Epirus Nicopolis, which had been founded by Augustus
in memory of his victory at Actium in 31 BC, grew to be a
considerable city. It was recognized, like Athens and Sparta,
as free and autonomous and must have had the fifth of the
votes in the Amphictyonic Confederacy. All these privileges
helped to swell the prosperity of the city. In addition games
were instituted there, the *Actia*, the victor at which received
the title of Actionices, and an "Actiad" calendar was introduced,
instead of the Olympiad.

Roman Administration

It was not, however, merely a case of the official recognition and, so to say, the imposition, of the Greek language
in the East (in the West, of course, Greek was not favoured,
but only Latin) in those areas where the barbarian danger
was most pressing. With their characteristic realism the Romans
perceived that by adopting this policy they not only performed
a service to their subjects but also prevented an entente
between the Greeks and the barbarians against themselves
and a revival, to some extent, of the western Asian ideas of
Mithridates. In imperial times particularly, the Romans
governed Greece itself in a different way from other countries.
They paid regard to Greek traditions and respected the
freedom and autonomy of the cities so beloved by the Greeks;
in doing so they had of course at the back of their minds
the consideration that thereby they were preventing a wider
understanding among the Greeks themselves. Even so, the
grant of self-government, or in some cases of some degree of

136 Mommsen. *op. cit.*, p. 202 ff., p. 279 ff.

exemption from taxation, was not universal; it was made only in return for services or obedience rendered to Rome. Without employing a uniform system of administration in the East, the Romans bestowed or revoked the privileges of autonomy as need and circumstances required. Vespasian, for example revoked many of the privileges which had been so liberally accorded to the Greeks by Nero.

Certain cities, like Sparta and Athens, which had been destroyed earlier by Sulla (86 BC), were shown special favour. Athens, in particular, struck its own coins without placing the Emperor's head upon them. Hadrian, besides his other benefactions, arranged for the provision of food supplies, which were mainly reserved for the cities of Italy. Athens came to be a "free state" under the Romans, as may be seen from the fact that the wealthy Athenian Julius Nicanor bought and presented to his fellow-citizens the island of Salamis.[137]

Ilion too (*Ilium Novum*), in the Troad, with which Rome had legendary connections, seems to have been granted tax-exemptions and perhaps other privileges as well.[138] But apart from the various privileges, greater or less, which were accorded to various cities, their union for certain purposes in "confederacies" may also be regarded as a sign of great favour. Thus the "Achaean Confederacy" was founded as early as the time of Augustus (who was also the founder of Patras), with its capital at Argos. In Hadrian's time this confederacy was reorganized and reentitled "Panhellenic," with its capital at Athens. Hadrian himself instituted new Games, the Panhellenia, at Athens.[139]

The Amphictyonic Confederacy was also refounded under the Empire with a religious significance. The "Intendant of the Amphictyonic Confederacy" was also called "Helladarch" and "High Priest of the August Gods" (i.e. the Emperors),

---

[137] Mommsen. *op. cit.*, Vol. V, p. 254 ff.

[138] V. Chapot. *Le Monde Romain*, p. 242.

[139] An inscription published in the
XXVII (1907), p. 148 reads "Titus Aelius . . . archon of the Panhellenic Synod of Athens, priest of the divine Hadrian, president of the great Panhellenia of the 18th Panhelleniad, first archon of the Panhellenes chosen by the most illustrious city of Thessalonice as Gymnasiarch and Chief Archon of that famous city."

which shows the religious significance of the Confederacy.[140] Similarly, we have a Macedonian Confederacy with its capital at Berrhoea; a Cretan Confederacy;[141] a Cyprian Confederacy;[142] a Confederacy of the Free Laconians with its capital at Gytheum, where, again, special Games, the Euryclean [143] and Caesarian, were celebrated; the "Confederacy of the Greeks in Asia" or the "Confederacy of Asia;" the "Confederacy of the Cities of the Province of Thrace," which was directed by the "Thraciarch" (Θρακάρχου); [144] the Confederacy of the Galatians; the Confederacy of the Lycians; the Confederacy of the Thessalians.[145]

Permission to found a temple and to set up a statue to the Emperor was also regarded as a privilege [146] from the time of Augustus onwards. The Emperor might refuse this concession. The official in charge of the temples and of the worship of the Emperor came to be the supreme representative of Rome in the provinces and was called High Priest, or more particular-

---

140 But the head of the Achaean Confederacy was also called High Priest and Helladarch, apparently because he supervised the worship of the Emperors.

141 M. van der Mijnisbrugge. *The Cretan KOINON*, 1931.

142 K. Spyridakis. *Cyprian Studies* (in Greek), Vol. II (1938), p. 31.

143 S. Kougeas, "Contributions to the History of Laconia from Inscriptions at Gytheum," in *Hellenika*, Vol. I (1928), p. 7 ff.

144 See the periodical   , Vol. VI (1935), p. 148, (*ibid.* on pp. 151 & 159 are to be found "the Rhodope tribe." and the Evros (Hebrus) tribe."

145 Th. Axenides. *Pelasgian Larissa and Ancient Thessaly* (in Greek), 1947.

146 Julius Caesar was the first to seek apotheosis, probably after the example of Alexander's successors: he was given the title *divus* by the Senate after his death. His kinsman Octavius regarded himself as the successor of Julius Ceasar and was therefore called *divi filius*, and was later given by the Senate the title of *Augustus* (Greek Σεβαστὸς This was likewise a religious title. Later, he also became *Pontifex Maximus* as the supreme religious authority. At Rome .Augustus did not seek deification, but in the provinces, and above all in the East, he allowed temples to be built jointly to the goddess Rome and to himself and worship to be conducted in them according to a prescribed form. At Rome the posthumous deification of Emperors after death was established as a custon by the Senate: it was regarded as a means of reinforcing the *Imperium Romanum*.

ly, Asiarch, Bithyniarch, Galatarch, Pontarch (in the Confederation of the Hexapolis on the Bulgarian coast), Macedoniarch or
Lyciarch. The grant of other official positions in the imperial
cult, as for instance that of Sacristan (νεώκορος), was
likewise regarded as a Roman favour.

Like self-government or other privileges, the dignity of
High Priest or Sacristan was bestowed on cities or taken from
them by the grace of the Emperor or according to the services
it had rendered to Rome. The Romans were thus enabled to
govern the Greek East after its own traditions, often by means
of a grant of autonomy which had at least this to recommend it,
that it delivered the Greeks from subordinate Roman officials.

Nevertheless, during the period of Roman sovereignty over
the Greeks, there developed among them a warmer affection
for their own country and attempts were made by private
individuals to assist it and to supply the need of a mother
state of their own. Just as at the time of the Turkish domination
the Greeks established schools and other useful foundations,
for which the Turkish Empire showed no concern, so too they
did in Roman times. We learn daily from inscriptions that
rich Greeks used to leave endowments for communal and
purely national objects. We have, for example, instances of
endowments for the apportionment and distribution of food or
alms to the poor;[147] for libraries, for the purchase of books, for
the observance of certain traditional ceremonies, dances [148]
and so forth. The Greeks could not fail, under Roman rule, to
carry on the example set by their forefathers—an example
unique in history of liberality in the public interest, in aid
of the fleet (the 'trierarchies'), athletic prowess, the theatre
and other causes.

---

[147] B. Laum. *Stiftungen in der griechischen und römischen Antike*, (1914),
Vol. II 100; *J.H.S.* Vol. LVII (1937), p. 1 ff.

[148] Laum. *op. cit.*, II, 23; Rostovtzeff (*Gesellschaft and Wirtschaft*, p. 125)
observes: " . . . it is striking what large sums were given by rich citizens,
especially to the Greek Orient. We know of hundreds of donations all
over Greece and Asia Minor."

CHAPTER VI

THE RELIGIONS OF THE EAST

Greek Religion

The Greeks of Old Greece had been distinguished by their lack of fanaticism [149] and of a priestly system. The great poets and philosophers — Homer, Hesiod, Aeschylus and others — had moulded Greek religion, and for this reason it had not the same inflexibility and dogmatic tone as the religions of Israel or Persia. Greek rationalism with its critical approach proved in time to be a solvent of the older religious conceptions and admitted new influences. Polytheism, pantheism and monotheism are all to be met with in ancient Greece, which without a trace of Jewish intolerance accepted the Thracian Dionysus or the Phrygian Sabazius, the cult of Orpheus, the mysteries of the earth-goddesses of Eleusis and of the Cabeiri of Samothrace. Only at Eleusis was there an organized priesthood,[150] a feature which was not transferred to any other Greek cult. The cult of Orpheus (which exercised an indirect influence upon Christianity) had no specific centre (τελεστηριον) , although from an early date philosophers like Pythagoras, Empedocles and Plato attached great value to its system of purifications and fasts. The Orphic initiates were the first Greek ascetics and the Orphic cult was related to that of Dionysus Lyaeus, who was in some sense a redeemer of the human soul.[151] From about the sixth century BC Orphism

---

[149] Th. Zielinski—A. Fichelle. *Ia religion de la Grece Antique*, 1926, p. 84.

[150] O. Kern. *Die Griechischen Mysterien der Klassichen Zeit*, 1927, p. 58.

[151] On Orphism in later times see A. Boulanger. *Orphée Rapports de l'Orphéisme et du Christanisme*, 1925. It is significant of the association of Orphism with Christianity in the minds of simple men that Alexander Severus was said to have had statues of Christ and Orpheus side by side in his palace.

gradually fostered in Greece the non-Greek idea of the redemption of the soul from the body, which took on such
importance in later times. Consequently, abstention from meat,
purity and even the punishment of sinners after death were
Orphic doctrines.[152]

Pythagoras

Orphism, with its fasts (abstention from meat, eggs and
beans) and its purifications, was regarded by Pythagoras as a
suitable instrument for the extension of his Order of ὁμάκοοι
or fellow students (a kind of Freemasonry) and he welcomed
it to the city of Crotona. Pythagoras was more the
founder of a religious order than a philosopher.[153] The Pythagoreans were indeed more given to the cultivation of philosophy and it was the Neopythagoreans who were more devoted
to the asceticism of their founder. Among the followers of
Pythagoras fanaticism was cultivated among Greeks for the
first time and this fanaticism was of great assistance to the
city of Crotona, where the order of Pythagoras was founded,
in defeating and overthrowing Crotona's rival, Sybaris. After
the overthrow of Sybaris, however, the Crotoniates did not
rest content with the aristocracy which Pythagoras had
supported, but desired a more democratic constitution. Differences then arose and Pythagoras was forced to fly from the
city.[154]

In Greece proper, where the rationalism of Socrates and

---

[152] Lietzmann. *Die Antike*, Vol. VIII (1932), p. 271.

[153] O. Spengler. *Der Untergang des Abendlandes. Umrisse einer Mor-
phologie der Weltgeschichte*, Vol I (1923), p. 373: "Pythagoras was not a
philosopher . . . he was a saint, a prophet and the founder of a fanatical
religious order which imposed its peculiar doctrines on its neighbours by
all available means, political and military."

[154] Some remarks may be noted from the Neoplatonist Porphyrius who
wrote a life of Pythagoras: "He was exceedingly fond of his friends, and
was first to declare that 'friends have all things in common' and that 'a
friend is another self." When they were in health he spent all his time
with them; when they were in bodily pain he healed them and comforted
their minds in sickness . . . some with charms and spells, others with
music." (A. Nauck. *Porphyrii philosophi platonici Opuscula selecta*, 1886,
Ch. 33; *Ibid.*, Chap. 46: "Mind of itself seeth all things and heareth all

the Sophists had flourished, there had meanwhile grown up a freedom of worship, which had not, as it never has, anything to do with rationalism but was solely a matter of sentiment or feeling. In religion, as Goethe said, "all is feeling." At the same time, through the Eleusinian and Orphic mysteries and through the Pythagoreans, the first elements of mysticism were unobtrusively introduced and these in their turn prepared the way for the direction of Greek thoughts towards the East, where oriental religion with all its mystic rites and its mystical outlook was destined to stifle Greek rationalism. As Zielinski says, [155] "We are left in amazement at the enthusiasm with which Greek thought rushes upon its own destruction (i.e. by adopting Asiatic cults) and at the frenzy with which it wrecks the fairest of its own creations, the noblest thing it had wrought since the time when it first appeared on earth."

We must now examine briefly the religious situation in the East, which the policy of Alexander and his successors had wished to leave completely undisturbed, since they had not foreseen that through its agency Greek civilization would lose its virtue and would be enslaved by the conquered East in the bonds of religion, just as, in Europe, on the contrary, conquered Greece through its higher civilization vanquished victorious Rome.

The Phrygian Gods

The deities of Asia Minor, Phrygian and others, had little influence on the Greeks. Already, before the time of Alexander, various Greek communities had adopted Sabazius, Cybele,

things: all else is deaf and blind.")

Pythagoras had a great effect on the legislation of Magna Graecia, since his disciples and admirers were great lawgivers. According to Iamblichus (Iamblichus. *De vita pythagorica liber*, ed. C. Deubner, 1937, p. 96) : "The followers of Pythagoras have been the best of all lawgivers. first Harondas of Catanis, then Zaleucus and Timaratus who drew up the laws of the Locrians, and besides these Theaetetus and Helikaon and Aristocrates and Photius who became the lawgivers of Rhegium." On the legislative achievement of the Greeks in Italy and its influence on Rome was great indeed. On the influence of the Pythagorean philosophy on Christianity see *Byzantion*, Vol. VI. (1931), p. 932.

[155] Zielinski. *op. cit.*, p. 168.

Agdistis, Attis, Bendis and other divinities, who won their own congregations (θίασοι) of worshippers in Greece. At the beginning of the third century BC the image of Cybele was transported to Rome from Pessinus in Phrygia, and it was to correspond with the Phrygian religious festival of March 25th that the date of the Christian festival of the Resurrection was subsequently fixed.[156] In Greek hands these Phrygian deities became milder and more rational and their insensate 'orgies' were toned down and became less unnatural. In these circumstances the Phrygian gods could hardly enslave the Greeks. Besides the Phrygian cults there was at Komana in Cappadocia the temple of the goddess Ma (the Roman Bellona) with thousands of servitors: this in itself had no effect on the Greeks,[157] but it does show that even in Asia Minor the latter did not venture to attack the native religion or even to abolish the slavery and the social degradation of the victims of the Cappadocian temples.

Zoroastrianism

One religion which exercised a great influence and might well have imposed itself upon the world, had it not been for the coming of Christianity, was that of Persia, Zoroastrianism, more particularly in its latter form, the cult of Mithras-Helios. Zoroaster probably lived and taught at the beginning of the sixth century BC (or earlier, according to some authorities), but it was Darius who made it the state religion. Its chief tenets were as follows. A continual struggle is in progress in the world between good and evil, light and darkness, represented by the god Ahura-Mazda (Ormuzd) and the evil Ahriman. In the end the good will prevail and those who have fought on its side will be rewarded: the soul, therefore, is immortal and there is a paradise for those who have braved the fight. The struggle in the cause of good in-

---

[156] W. Nestle. *Griechische Religiosität von Alexander dem grossen bis auf Proklos,* 1934, p. 43.

[157] Even so, we learn from an inscription (*Athena,* Vol.. XII (1906) p. 65) that at Edessa in Macedonia there was a temple of "the sovereign goddess Ma, the Unconquerable, the Hearer of Prayer," with a multitude of temple slaves.

cludes also the cultivation of the earth and the supervision of nomadism which was a scourge of ancient Persia.[158] Particulars of ancient Zoroastrianism were later, in Sassanid times, collected in the book known as Avesta and its commentaries, known as the Pehlevis. Under the inspiration of this religion, the Persian kings, Darius and his successors, waged a long series of campaigns. The Greeks came to know certain aspects of Zoroastrianism through Asia Minor: Heraclitus and Plato, in the *Timaeus*, were already familiar with some of its doctrines.

Zoroastrianism greatly influenced the Jews, who became familiar with it during the Exile in Babylon, to which they had been transported by Nebuchadnezzar (596-586 BC). Those who returned to Judaea in 525 BC after their liberation by Cyrus carried with them the ideas of redemption, of Paradise, of an evil spirit or Satan, and of a Second Coming, which passed through Judaism into Christianity. [159]

Later on, in the time of the Arsacids, Zoroastrianism became linked with the Semitic astrology of the Chaldeans and in this altered shape, as the cult of Mithras-Helios, it was spread under the name of Mithraism all over the ancient, especially the Roman, world by the soldiery, whose enthusiasm was roused by its fighting spirit. Greek civilization resisted Mithraism for racial reasons, since it resisted every activity of Persian origin. Leaving Greece, then, out of account,[160] in the East there was a particularly strong rapprochement between Mithraism and the Greek gods, so that in the celebrated inscription of Antiochus at Commagene we find among other things:

> The great King, Antiochus, the Just God,
> The Manifest, Lover of Rome and Lover of the Greeks.

(v. 11)   Above all virtues I consider *piety* to be not only the surest of possessions but the sweetest of enjoyments.

(v. 55)   Therefore, as thou seest, I caused to be set up these godlike statues of Zeus Oromasdes and Apollo Mithras,

---

[158] I. Kaerst. *Geschichte des Hellenismus*, 3rd ed. Vol. I. (1927), p. 555.

[159] E. Meyer. *Ursprung und Anfänge des Christentums*, Vol. II. (1921), p. 51.

[160] In certain Greek cities of Asia Minor, Trebizond for example, the figure of Mithras was placed on the coinage.

of Helios Hermes and Artagnus (?) Heracles, of
Ares and of my fruitful country Commagene.[161]

In this inscription, so typical in its 'piety', Oromasdes is
equated with Zeus, and Mithras with Apollo, In others Mithras
is Helios, as for example in *JGSJ*, Art. 891: "To Helios Mithras,
the Unconquered."

The Greeks, then—except those of Greece proper—and
those who had adopted Greek civilization were familiar with
Mithras, but it was the Roman soldiers who were the apostles
of Mithraism in the Roman Empire. After the defeat of Zenobia
and the dissolution of the kingdom of Palmyra in 247 AD, the
Emperor Aurelian officially introduced the cult of the "Unconquered Sun" (*Sol Invictus*), the general predominance of
which only Christianity was able gradually to reduce.[162] Not
even Julian's attempt to combine Mithraism with the ancient
Greek religion was fated to succeed.

Mazdek later evolved a new form of Mithraism and transformed it into a kind of communism by introducing community
of women and property.

Mithraism also had a great influence upon Manichaeism,
the founder of which, Manes of Ctesiphon (215-276 AD), sought
to combine Christianity with the Persian religion. Manes was
persecuted by the Sassanids, and his doctrine was persecuted
both by the Persians and by Orthodox Christianity, but his
influence in Asia was nevertheless great, owing above all to
his asceticism and to his practice of temperance in all its
forms. The Manichees, and later the Nestorians, often spread
Christian ideas in Asiatic lands which Orthodox Christianity
was unable to penetrate.

Most Greeks, as has been said, did not worship Mithras;
nevertheless, certain features of Mithraism, such as the purifications (not the special rites of the ταυροβόλια [bull sacri-

---

[161] Jalabert-Mouterde. *Inscriptions Grecques et Latines de la Syrie*, Vol. I.
(1929), p. 13 ff.

[162] On Zoroastrianism and its later development Mithraism and their
influence, see E. Meyer. *op. cit.*, Vol. II, p. 50 ff.; Cl. Huart. *La Perse
antique et la civilisation iranienne*, 1925, pp. 139, 208, 211 ff.; Reitzenstein-
Schaeder. *Studien zum antiken Synkretismus - Aus Iran und Griechenland*.
1926, p. 125, 147; Fr. Cumont. *Les religions orientales dans le paganisme
romain*. 4th ed. 1929, p. 148 ff.

fices) and κριοβόλια [ram sacrifices] but the purification by fire and water), the fasts and prayers, as also the idea of the immortality of the soul after death, reinforced the propagation of similar doctrines by other religions. Christianity, as has been said, received a number of these doctrines through Judaism; and later on Mohammedanism, which was to destroy Mithraism in the land of its birth, adopted several of its doctrines in Sufism, the mystical theosophy which separated the believer from the world without, however, condemning him to impassivity and annihilation.

The Worship of the Sun

In Greece sun worship had been widespread from ancient times and the sun had been adored at his rising and setting. The statue of Helios at Rhodes is world-famed and there are many well-known hymns to the sun, as also to the moon.[163] In inscriptions the sun is termed "Surveyor of all things" (παντεπόπτης), "Governor of the whole world." An inscription from Syria runs: "I call upon thee, Lord Sun. I beseech thee, Lord Sun, hear me." [164] In the *Aethiopica* of Heliodorus the words occur, ". . . your ancestral god Apollo, who also is the Sun." According to the philosopher Posidonius the sun is the creator of the world. In Rome the worship of the sun was imported in the course of the third century AD from the East, where the Greeks too had found confirmation for their own original religious ideas on this subject. Heliogabalus brought to Rome the statue of the sun from Emesa in Syria, and Aurelian officially recognized the cult. Mithraism, the cult of Mithras who was also equated with the sun, reinforced this new official religion of the Roman Empire,[165] of which the Emperor Julian remained a devout adherent. Constantine himself retained the effigy of the sun on the coins which he struck after 310; he too, therefore, must to some extent have been subject to the attraction of the cult.

---

[163] E. Miller. *Mélanges de littérature grecque*, Paris 1868, p. 44.

[164] *Syria.* 14. 392.

[165] See K. Pfister. *Der Untergang der antiken Welt*, 1941, p. 273.

Monotheism

From Syria, but in more ancient times, had come the worship of Adonis and Aphrodite-Astarte. The cult of Belus or Baal (i. e. the sun), who was equated with Mithras and the Greek Apollo, had no need to conduct special propaganda. Palestine, on the other hand, was the home of monotheism, the worship of Jehovah, which did not, however, spread outside the country. Monotheistic ideas were also prevalent in Greece, not only among the philosophers as a conclusion of philosophical research, but sometimes among the people as well; but they did not derive from Jewish monotheism, which was exclusive, purely Jewish and hostile to the outer world. The intolerant and fanatical character of Jewish monotheism can of course be explained by the special circumstances of Jewish history. When the Jews returned in humiliation from exile, they felt the need to rally round the national religion and organized themselves under their religious heads, the High Priests, as national leaders. Under a hierocratic system of this kind intolerance was bound to prevail. When Antiochus Epiphanes (175-164) attempted to break the back of Jewish resistance by main force and to enforce a closer relation between the Jews and Greek culture, the Jews under the Maccabees began for the first time to struggle against Greek influence, which proved quite unable to produce any change in Jewish ways of thought.

The Essenes

Modern research, however, shows that one section of the population of Palestine (which was inhabited not only by Jews but also by Philistines, who had formerly come from ancient Crete and were of Indo-Germanic origin) came under the influence of the teachings of Pythagoras and the Neopythagoreans. This sect, or rother order, was that of the Essenes, who held their property in common, owned no slaves, did not engage in trade, practiced agriculture and worshipped the sun.[166]

---

[166] Fr. Cumont. "Esseniens et Pythagoriens d'apres un passage de Josephe," *Académie des Inscriptions et Belles Letters*, Paris 193-, p. 96. On the Essenes see also G. Walter. *Les Origines du Communisme*, 1931, p. 52.

(Josephus, *Jewish Antiquities*. III, 1, 5: ". . . the Essenes are the best in their way of life: all their efforts are directed to agriculture . . . and the rich man enjoys no more of the necessaries of life than he who owns nothing: and more than four thousand men practise this creed.") Cumont accepts as accurate another passage of Josephus, according to which "this community follows the diet laid down among the Greeks by Pythagoras." Modern investigators have shown that the ideas of the Neopythagoreans had reached Palestine through the Jews of Egypt and they have drawn attention to the similarity between many phrases of the Pythagorean texts and the Gospels, and from this they have been led to agree that the tales concerning Jesus must have been spread into Essene circles. Certain Jewish strata, therefore, did not escape Greek influence.

Egyptian Gods

Finally, a few words may be added on the divinities borrowed from Egypt. The Greeks in that country, the home of centuries of blind superstition, did not dare to proceed against Egyptian religion, even to the extent they had proceeded against the Jews. Under Greek rule the Egyptian priests continued undisturbed the work of their religion in exploiting and blinding the Egyptian people. The Greeks not only did not alter the religious situation but themselves adopted the worship of Isis and Serapis, whom they equated with the Greek deities Demeter and Zeus or Asclepius (Aesculapius). As already noted, Bryaxis made a statue of Zeus-Serapis and introduced a Greek version of the Egyptian god. The Ptolemies founded a temple of Serapis at Alexandria, the great Serapeum, and an Iseum at Philae. In Greece, too, and at Tome, the worship of Serapis, and still more of Isis, became widespread and there were many temples of both divinities. Plutarch wrote on Isis, many Greek hymns were written to her, [167] and there are many mentions in inscriptions of the new gods

[167] W. Peck. *Der Isis-Hymnus von Andros und verwandte Texte*, 1930. The orator Aelius Aristides wrote a "Praise of Serapis" (ed. Keil. Vol II (1898), p. 352, No. XLV) and expresses the belief that "whatever regulates and preserves the life of man is the work of Serapis." Aristides also says: "In every extremity all men call thee to their aid, Serapis."

from Egypt. A frequent dedication is "To Zeus Helios, the great Serapis" (e.g. *JGSL*, art. 915, 1031, and elsewhere). The following inscription is also typical in its simultaneous reference to Isis, Serapis and the Ptolemies as gods:

> "To King Ptolemy and Queen Berenice, divine
> benefactors, and to Isis, Serapis and Harpocrates,
> Taurinus son of Heracleus." [168]

Chaldean Astrology

The observations made above show that through its religion the East was attempting gradually to invade its Greek and Roman invaders. The Greeks directly rejected Mithraism, but indirectly they came under the influence of the Mithraic mysteries, as they did under that of other cults of Asia Minor, Syria and Egypt. The astrology of the Chaldeans afforded them a certain amount of astronomical knowledge and probably assisted the work of the great astronomers Aristarchus and Hipparchus; but it also helped to spread the mystical point of view by its doctrine that human destiny was greatly dependent on the stars and not, in consequence, on the activity of man himself, which not only Greek rationalism but Zoroastrianism as well had sought to promote. [169]

Astrology with its associated arts of prophecy also influenced the great Posidonius himself and he was responsible for spreading it further. For this same reason the Stoic Posidonius is regarded as the man who reconciled Eastern theology with Greek philosophy and who was on that account listened to on all sides and became a universal influence.

Magical Papyri

Like every narcotic of the mind, Chaldean astrology found

---

[168] W. Dittenberger. *Orientis Graeci Inscriptiones Selectae.* 1903, No. 62. In Cumont (*op. cit.*) the following inscription is noted on p. 79: "To Zeus, Serapis, Helios, Lord of the World, the Unconquered."

[169] The good and evil influences of the various stars are reflected in the names given in Roman and later times to the days of the week: *Solis dies* (Sunday), *Lunae dies* (Monday), etc.

a particularly fruitful soil in benighted Egypt,[170] where it undertook by magic and prediction to rescue man, even during his earthly existence, from sickness and other evils, whereas the mysteries of the other different cults merely promised to save his soul after death. The innumerable magical papyri which have been found show that from the first century BC onwards the Greeks of Egypt ceased to bear any resemblance to their predecessors of the third century BC, the creators of the great mathematical, philological and medical science of Alexandria. From the first century BC the Egyptian Greeks descended to the level of the Egyptians themselves, who were ready to believe any foolishness in the name of religion. The magical papyri of Egypt, with their adjurations, their spells, their enquiries about the future, show that scientific knowledge was already a thing of the past, and that astrology and the mysteries had already brought in the Middle Ages, which believed most devoutly the kind of thing we find in these papyri. A few texts may here be picked out, perhaps, from the collection of Preisendanz [171] (Vol. II, p. 131) : "I adjure thee, by the holy name, to heal Dionysius . . . , son of Heraclia, from all chills and fever, whether daily or single, whether by night or by day or quaternian, now, now, quickly, quickly." (Vol. II, p. 157) : "To Zeus-Helios, the great Serapis and those that share his temple: Nike asks whether I should buy from Tasarapion the slave Sarapion he has and the slave Gaion: grant me this." (Vol. II, p. 9.) : "For a feverish chill take oil in thy hands and say seven 'Sabaoths' twice alond and anoint thyself from the base of the spine to the feet." I add a part of the following text for its language (Vol. I, p. 94) : "Hail, Lord, mighty in power, mighty Ruler and King, greatest of gods, Helios, Lord of heaven and earth, god of gods, thy breath is strength, thy power is strength, Lord . . . " [172]

This Greek civilization of the magical papyri was no

---

[170] U. Wilamowitz-Moellendorff. *Der Glaube der Hellenen*, Vol. II (1932), p. 401.

[171] K. Preisendanz. *Papyri Graecae Magicae*, Vols. I & II, 1928-31.

[172] Besides the magical papyri, another source of information on the foolishness which had taken possession of Egypt is the so-called "Hermetic" books which have been published under the title *Hermetica* by W. Scott (Vols. I-III, Oxford 1924-26). See too A. Noek — A. Festugiere. *Corpus*

longer capable of directing the world, nor were its Roman
successors, as we shall see.

The Enslavement of Greek Culture to Religion

It is accepted today by modern research [173] that Greek
civilization, after conquering the East (including Egypt) was
enslaved by the religions of the East and ceased to rule it:
it shaped its course towards the Dark Ages. As Lehmann said,
"Mysticism destroyed the ancient world." [174] The Egyptians
and the other peoples of the Orient were tortured into this
view of life by their kings, their priests, their conquerors
and their men of wealth, and had no hope of ever finding
salvation upon earth. They therefore became adherents of
religion and sought salvation from that source, even if only
after death. All these religions insisted on certain secret
(mystic) or public rites, fasting, purifications and so forth,
and promised the faithful redemption after death. The conception of the body as the prison-house of the soul, the
withdrawal from the community, the ideas of sin, repentance
and punishment were Eastern notions which also penetrated
to some extent into the Neoplatonic philosophy and into
Christianity. Baptism as a means of purification was in use
even before Christianity.[175] Blind faith was sufficient to save.

Hermeticum, Paris 1945. In the second century AD there came to birth under
the influence of Chaldean astrology the worship of the Egyptian god·Thoth
(whom the Greek settlers called Hermes Trismegistos), which cultivated
intensively the hope of redemption after death. See the article "Hermes
Trismegistos," in the *RE*, and A. Festugiere. *La révelation d'Hermes
Trismegistos*, Vol. II, Paris 1949.

[173] Out of the enormous literature on the subject I mention a few of the
easier and better studies: W. Schubart. "Hellenismus und Weltreligion,"
Neue Jahrbücher für Wissenschaft und Jugendbildung, Vol. II (1926), p.
505; H. Lietzmann. "Das Problem der Spätantike," *Sitzungsberichte der
Berliner Akademie Philosoph. Hist. Classe* (1927), p. 342. H. Schaeder.
"Der Orient und das Griechische Erbe," in *Die Antike*, Vol. IV (1928) p.
226. R. Reitzenstein. *Die Hellenistiche Mysterienreligion nach ihren
Grundgedanken und Wirkungen*, 3rd ed. 1927.

[174] E. Lehmann. *Mystik und Christentum*, 9th ed. 1923, p. 2: "In Mystik
ist die Antike untergegangen.'

[175] See Taufe in *RE* and A. Rahmer. *Griechische Mythen in Christlicher
Deutung*, 1945, p. 101.

According to Clement of Alexandria (*Fragments*, I, p. 261),
"And some there are that think themselves clever who claim
that they will not touch philosophy nor even learn the contem-
plation of nature, and they require bare faith alone." According to another formula, "to think is to believe and not to
believe is not to think." This abandonment of the individual
to the mercy of God was encouraged by the economic decline
and the maladministration of the Roman Empire and these
two factors help us to understand the origins of the Middle
Ages and of the religious chaos which Christianity reduced
to order.

Christianity

The social degradation caused by the Roman conquest and
the confusion of religions caused by the existence of so
many forms of worship in the East prepared the way for the
appearance of a new and higher religion, Christianity. Two
factors helped to promote the advance of Christianity with
such great rapidity [176] and against all opposition: 1) the
coalescence of various cults in the time of Christ, and the
fact that certain features were common to many Eastern
religions, as for example the ascetic life (abstention from
meat), purifications, belief in salvation after death, the practice of various mysteries, etc. The Orphics, in particular,
prepared the way for Christianity by their austere way of
living and their mysteries. 2) Again, the social situation and
the maladministration of the Roman Empire reduced the
lowest strata of the population to a pitiful state of distress.
The Roman officials and the rich exploited and degraded the
poor to an unbelievable degree and it was an easy matter to
secure them for a religion which not only instructed them
from the most elementary stage and based itself solely upon
love but also in the early Christian ages practiced a philanthropy and a concern for social welfare which were unique.

As Eduard Meyer says: [177] "When states decline religions
flourish." The history of the theocratically ruled peoples of
the East shows clearly that when men have despaired of

[176] The first pagan evidence about Christ is that of Tacitus (117 AD).

[177] E. Meyer. *Blüte und Niedergang des Hellenismus in Asien*, 1925, p. 76.

finding justice and happiness on earth they take refuge in a quest for salvation from God.

The spread of Christianity, a religion so inimical to the Roman Empire, is a clear proof that despite the famous organizing ability and conquering power of Rome, the Empire was doomed to decline. The more peoples Rome conquered, the more rapidly it became corrupted itself and corrupted its subjects.

Those who condemn many of the techniques of Christianity forget that it was in the first place a reaction against Rome. The Christian emphasis on virginity, for example, was a reaction against Roman prostitution and vice. W. Otto was wrong when he wrote that "the triumph of Christianity is the most deplorable event in the history of European thought. The Christian scale of values, according to which pride is the supreme sin and humility the supreme virtue, reduced human morality to its lowest level." [178] Clearly this brilliant historian of antiquity had not observed that Christianity was a reaction.

The Gospel of Equality and Love

Unnoticed by Rome, in a corner of the East, in the monotheistic home of the Jews, a new religion was born with an intensely Messianic creed and, above all, with a burning gospel of love. This religion dared to tell Rome to its face, through the greatest of its preachers, Paul, that "There is neither Jew nor Greek, there is neither bond nor free, there is neither male nor female: for ye are all one in Christ Jesus." (*Gal.* III, 28) [179] But these notions of the equality of men and

[178] W. Otto. *Der Geist der antiken und die christliche Welt*, 1923, pp. 79 and 110.

[179] Paul was content to teach the equality of slaves and freemen. He made no more systematic attack on slavery. On the contrary, in the first *Epistle to Timothy* (VI, 1) he particularly enjoins obedience to masters, and he charges all, "Let as many servants as are under the yoke count their own masters worthy of all honour." To the Corinthians he writes (I *Cor.* VII, 20): "Let every man abide in the same calling wherein he was called. Art thou called, being a servant care not for it . . . For he that is called in the Lord being a servant, is the Lord's freeman." The words of Paul may be explained by the kindly attitude of Christians in those times towards their slaves, but also by the idea that in the eyes of the Lord slave and freemen were alike. On the attitude and the mutual love of Christians, see Paul's *Epistle to the Romans*, XII, 9.

women, of Romans and other peoples were as offensive and distasteful to Rome as they were honorable and comfortable to the poor and humble. Again, the Messianic conceptions of Christianity with regard to the end of the world and salvation after death through the Kingdom of Heaven were subversive in the eyes of Rome, but consoling to those in bondage. The Christian gospel, therefore, spread by enthusiastic missionaries like Paul and his fellow apostles, found an echo in the racked peoples of the East, who had, besides, been prepared for it by the coalescence of religions taking place at that time. But even more than the doctrines of equality and of the salvation of man after death, the spread of Christianity was aided by the pattern of the martyrdom of Christ, by the gospel of love, by the solidarity, the brotherly feeling, the forgiveness, the compassion of Christians. The disciples of Christ and their disciples copied Christ's own life of self-denial, they were ready to bear him witness and they put into practice his teaching on the love they should bear each other. The first Christians were "brethren," they held nearly all their goods in common,[180] they distributed food and money to the poor, they cared for widows and orphans, they ransomed prisoners. Ignatius, Bishop of Antioch, accuses the opponents of Christianity of inhumanity: "Ye know the infidels . . . how they are contrary to the will of God. They have no care for love, nor for widows, nor for the orphans, nor for those in tribulation, nor for the bond or the free, nor for them that hunger and thirst."[181] A typical feature of early Christianity was the *agape*, a gathering for a communal meal, prayer and edification, which was a wonderful medium for evangelization and for the regeneration of men. With such a spirit of mutual love and mutual aid, Christianity could not fail to spread rapidly among slaves and bondmen, among the poor and those who

---

[180] *Acts* II, 44-47: "And all that believed were together, and had all things common; and sold their possessions and goods and parted them to all men, as every man had need." Elsewhere, too (*Acts*. IV, 32-36): "Neither was there any among them that lacked; for as many as were possessors of lands or houses sold them, and brought the prices of the things that were sold, and laid them down at the apostles' feet: and distribution was made unto every man according as he had need."

[181] *Epistle of Ignatius to the Smyrnaeans*, 6.

suffered injustice from the rich, and finally among idealists of the upper classes (of whom there are always some in the world) although these had no immediate need of Christian aid. Philanthropic work constituted the essence of Christianity and advanced its cause long before its doctrinal aspect had been elaborated, whether the Christological or the ideological.[182] This philanthropic activity not only created the Christianity of the early centuries and spread it throughout the world but also maintained its power through the Middle Ages. In the fourth century the first hospitals were founded by Ephraim the Syrian in the East and by the widow Fabiola in the West. Under the legislation of Constantine and Justinian the philanthropic work of the Church was better organized. We cannot understand the expansion and the power of monastic life at Byzantium and in the West unless we realize the philanthropic activity of the monasteries.[183] Similarly, we shall not understand the influence of certain monks, bishops and even statesmen—Saint Antony, for example, Theodore of Studium and others — if we do not know this humane side of their lives.

In these circumstances it can easily be understood that the Christians, with their strong sense of solidarity, did not fear the contempt or hatred or the persecutions of the heathen and were ready even to undergo martydom for their new social and religious creed.

The Clash between Christianity and Rome

Christianity did in fact amount to an insurrection against Rome, as also against the domination of wealth and against the old religions. Christians took no part in the ancient sacrifices but practiced their own rites, usually apart and in

182 On the philanthropic activity of Christianity see the University address of Prof. A. Alivizatos. "The social mission of the Church," 1925 (in Greek); the articles "Agape," "Charite" and "Hopitaux" in Cabrol-Leclerq, Dictionaire d'Archéologie Chretienne et de Liturgie; A. Harnack, *Die Mission und Ausbreitung des Christentums*, 4th ed. (1924), Vol. II. p. 170. Also Pöhlmann-Certal. *Geschichte der socialen Frage und des Socialismus in der antiken Welt*, Vol. IV (1942), p. 464. For the essential features of Christianity see A. Harnack's study *Das Wesen des Christentums*, 1926.

183 See K. Amantos. "Greek Philanthropy in the Middle Ages," (in Greek) in *Athena*, Vol. XXXV (1923), p. 132 ff.

secret, in catacombs and other hiding places. They were consequently looked upon as atheists and were often misrepresented as immoral. The interests of the ancient temples and their priests were injured by the abstention and the opposition of the Christians. The Christian conception of the end of the world was regarded by many as a threat to the Roman Empire, the downfall of which it in a sense foretold. The slaves and freemen who were otherwise defenseless in the face of the Roman state found support in the Church, which even recognized marriages which the state did not. Many Christians evaded conscription and thus in a sense defied the state. But it was especially the refusal of Christians to acknowledge the worship of the Roman Emperor as the representative of Rome which led to the clash between Christianity and the Empire.

After the manner of the ancient Greeks, the ancient Romans had not been fanatical in matters of religion. They had taken over gods from the Greeks and had altered the personalities of Roman gods to fit the Greek mythology. They had welcomed the cult of Mithras, which Roman soldiers had introduced and which had been officially recognized by the Emperor Aurelian, who had engraved on his coinage the image of the Unconquered Sun, with whom Mithras was equated. Caracalla recognized the cult of Isis, to whom Apuleius addressed his prayers. In the course of their wars with Mithridates, the ruler of Pontus, the Roman soldiery had adopted and spread the savage cult of Ma, goddess of the Comanians, whom the Romans had retitled Bellona and whose resident priests (*fanatici*) thenceforward gave their name to all intolerant religious sectaries.

But all these religions and cults, whether recognized by the state or not, had a limited number of adherents and limited congregations and presented no danger to the state. Their followers maintained no contemptuous or active opposition to any article of state belief or any state activity. The worship of Mithras-Helios, as conceived by the monotheistically-minded Aurelian, was intended to become supreme, but this supremacy was not pursued to the detriment of other religions.

In the face of the varied religions and creeds of its subject peoples, Rome had wished before Aurelian's time to follow the example of the Seleucids and Ptolemies and to introduce the worship and apotheosis of the Emperor, not as an individual but as the representative of the state. Contempt of this cult and opposition to it were an attack on the majesty of the Roman people, a blasphemous offense. Those who like the Christians, refused to adore the Emperor were outside the law.

In spite of the clash between the Christians and the Empire over Emperor-worship, the Romans did not hasten to begin official persecution of them. Only here and there did minor persecutions, of greater or lesser severity, take place, as for instance the persecution under Nero (64 AD) at Rome, due to the burning of the city which was attributed to the Christians.[183] Similarly, there were limited persecutions of individuals or units by Roman officials or other pagans whose interests or ideas were offended by the stubbornness of Christian resistance. It is understandable that senior officials (and even emperors like Valerian, under whom St. Cyprian was martyred in North Africa in 258 AD) sought excuses for persecution in order to confiscate Christian property. Other bishops too were martyred at various dates, as for instance Ignatius of Antioch (107 AD), Sixtus of Rome (116-125) and Telesphorus (125-136) and Polycarp of Smyrna.

More general persecutions took place later, particularly from the reign of Decius onwards. The idea that the Christians were proving dangerous and injurious to the Roman Empire was a particular inducement to Decius, and later to Galerius and Diocletian, to institute persecutions against them.[184] But the persecutions showed that the solidarity of the Christians and their readiness to help each other had nothing to fear from them. Christians gladly underwent martyrdom since this reflected honour on themselves and their families, who were very well cared for in case of need by their brethren of the faith. The persecutions [185] tested and exalted their courage and thus contributed to the swifter expansion of Christianity.

[184] C. Papadopoulos. "The Roman state and Christianity down to the middle of the 3rd century," (in Greek) in *Theologia*, Vol. I (1923), p. 67 ff; Vol. II, p. 5. ff.

[185] On the Christian persecutions see E. Myer. *Ursprung und Anfänge des Christentums*, Vol. III. (1923), p. 510.

Expansion of the Christian Religion

As has been said, Christianity was born in Palestine and was in a sense a "fulfilment," a supplementation and correction of the ancient Jewish faith, as this had taken shape after the Exile and the return of the Jews to Palestine. It was adopted by many liberal-minded Jews but not by those who were conservative, orthodox and fanatical, who followed their ancestral traditions formally and strictly and did not approve the changing of a jot or a tittle. The appearance of Christianity once again put to the test the barren creed of extreme conservatism and showed that progress demands the adaptation of old ways of thought to new.

But if Christianity encountered resistance among conservative Jews despite its Jewish origin, the Greeks welcomed it with great eagerness in Syria and Asia Minor. The Greek κοινή (or "common" dialect) which was particularly the speech of the towns, was instrumental in spreading Christianity rapidly throughout the East, and partly, too, in spreading it to Rome and southern Gaul, to Lyons (Lugdunum) and elsewhere.[186] It is significant that in the first, and still more in the second, century there were so many Greek popes, Evarestus (97 AD), Alexander (105 AD), Telesphorus (125 AD), Hyginus and others. We can understand this more easily when we remember that a large number of Greek funeral inscriptions have been found in Rome dating from this period.

But not only the Greek language but Greek philosophy and the Greek view of life contributed to the strengthening and organization of Christianity: "The irruption of the Greek spirit," says Harnack, "and its alliance with the Gospel constitute the greatest event in the history of the Church in the second century."[187] If the earliest Christianity had been the "fulfilment" of Judaism, from the second century Christianity came under the influence of Platonic and Stoic philosophy and the Messiah or Christ himself was renamed the *Logos* in

---

186 On the expansion of Christianity in Asia Minor see C. Papadopoulos. *Asia Minor as the cradle of Greek Christian civilisation* (in Greek), 1919. The principal work on the expansion of Christianity is: A. Harnack. *Mission und Ausbreitung des Christentums*, 4th ed., 1924.

187 A. Harnack. *Das Wesen des Christentums*, 1926, p. 125.

Greek philosophical terms. Thus Christianity became Greek rather than Jewish and its Greek character helped its organization and expansion.

The world-empire of Rome did not succeed in imposing its language on early Christianity, the organization of which was "a Greek phenomenon." The noblest elements of the ethics of the Greek philosophers were absorbed into the new religion, whose first adherents were largely Greeks.[188]

Montanism

It has already been stated that Christianity was regarded as a dangerous enemy of the Roman Empire; but it was more particularly Montanism which in fact had its origin in detestation of the Roman state. Montanism was founded in the second century by Montanus of Phrygia, who may have been a priest of Cybele earlier in his career. He organized the movement as an order on which strict fasts and abstinences were imposed, together with the prohibition of remarriage, the virginity of the unmarried and an eagerness for martyrdom. The Montanists did not serve as Roman soldiers and, generally speaking, this religious heresy covered resistance to Rome and a kind of Phrygian nationalist organization.

Monasticism

Monastic life, again, received a great extension owing to opposition to the Roman Empire. In earlier times too there had been ascetics and those who practiced celibacy and virginity— the κάτοχοι of the Serapeum,[189] the θεραπευταί the Essenes to some extent. But in Egypt monastic life was to take a special form and show a special development, precisely because it was there that men suffered most at the hands of officials, usurers and other exploiters, Greek and Roman. Just as in the period of Turkish domination those who suffered in the towns fled to the mountains and founded monasteries or

---

188 See L. Quernet — A. Boulanger. Le génie grec dans la religion, 1932, p. 517 ff.

189 C. Papadopoulos. The κάτοχοι of the Serapeum at Memphis and the beginnings of monastic life in Egypt (in Greek), Vol. XII (1913), p. 450.

villages in inaccessible places, so the Egyptians fled to the deserts of Libya or Sinai to show their contempt and hatred for the worldly might of Rome. The early example set by the famous Egyptian monks gave a particular impulse to the development of monastic life. Antony, "an Egyptian by race . . . of gentle parents, who could live of their own," gave away part of his property to his friends and the rest to the poor and went into the desert. There he displayed great endurance and resistance to bodily suffering, to hunger and thirst, and his example attracted countless others to imitate him. He became a famous and exemplary figure through the biography written of him by St. Athanasius.[190]

Another celebrated monk, also an Egyptian, was Pachomius who in 318 founded the first coenobitic monastery in Egypt.

The Persians and Christianity

The persecutions of the Roman imperial power ceased in the days of Constantine and thenceforward the Church received an administrative organization. Christian literature developed freely and the resources of art were placed at its disposal and gradually evolved a special architectural style. Outside the Empire, however, Christianity was persecuted. As is well known, in Persia Christianity was regarded rather as an agency of the Roman Empire and was persecuted for that reason, while any Christians who were obliged to take refuge in Persia as heretics were kindly received because they were regarded as enemies of the romans.[191]

The Persian persecutions placed Byzantium in an awkward situation and helped towards the outbreak of more than one war. In their treaties with Persia the Byzantine emperors often included stipulations on behalf of Christians and intervened in their favour with the Sassanids at various times in return for various concessions, as Constantine himself did, for example, when he made over to the Persians a quantity of iron.

[190] Athanasius, bishop of Alexandria. "Life and conduct of our holy father Antony," Migne. *PG*, Vol. XXVI, p. 857.

[191] J. Zeiller. *L'empire romain et l'église*, 1927, p. 103.

CHAPTER VII

LITERATURE IN THE CHRISTIAN ERA

After the opening of the Christian era most of the creative writers came from the Greek communities of Asia and from Egypt. A brief survey is added here, to throw into clearer relief the significance of the Greek communities of the East. Even though the writers of the Christian era are seldom distinguished by great originality, there are nevertheless many among them who are of great value as having preserved the works and the traditions of older masters.

Greece

From the mother of all learning, ancient Greece, we have very few creative writers in Christian times. The chief is the great Boeotian, Plutarch of Chaeronea (48-120 AD), fellow-countryman of the ancients Hesiod and Pindar. Plutarch belonged to a distinguished family which for four generations had given valuable service to Greece. He had travelled widely, in Italy and Egypt, but was content to remain in his native country since he loved it dearly and desired to serve it. Plutarch was a Platonist but was influenced also by Posidonius. He was not enslaved by Atticism, which was the prevailing fashion of his time, nor by the art of rhetoric; he studied, indeed, the works of his predecessors, but he knew foreign literature as well, and it is this fact that makes his biographies of Greeks and Romans a work very typical of its author. He was religious, like his compatriots Hesiod and Pindar before him, and besides serving as priest in his native Chaeronea, he served also as a priest at Delphi. He studied and learned from the works of his forerunners in order to instruct his contemporaries, not so much in some specific system of philosophy as in the great examples which he assembles with much skill. As a biographer he pays a great deal of attention to facial characteristics and he was, besides, the first to make use of characteristic anecdotes, a feature which has assumed so much importance for many modern historians. Plutarch sets before us the old religion and the old civilization with an aim which is always instructive. Thereby, it is certain, he not only moulded many of the men of his own time—which was his object—but has had an effect on great scholars and poets of a later age, on Shakespeare, Montaigne and Goethe. Plutarch is a flower of Greek civilization which, as Mommsen said, could never flourish in the East. "He was as purely native as honey from Hymettus." [192] His nephew, the Stoic philosopher Sextus, became the teacher of Marcus Aurelius.

Herodes Atticus (191-177 AD) was a celebrated Sophist, a pupil of the Bithynian Aelius Aristides. In the third century there lived and worked in Athens the admirable historian Dexippus — accounted by Photius a peer of Thucydides — who helped to defend his country against the Goths.

From Macedonia and Thrace there were very few writers—Polyaenus (162 AD), who wrote on tactics, Eumenes of Cardia in the Thracian Chersonese and one or two more. Among later writers were Joannes Stobaeus (fifth century), the compiler of the famous Anthology, and Stephen of Byzantium who wrote the geographical dictionary known as the *Ethnica*.

Mathematicians, Medical Men, Grammarians, Philosophers

We must now examine the "pagan" writers from the East and Egypt, and after them the Christian writers. First of all, it should be mentioned that in the third century there flurished at Alexandria the famous mathematician Diophantus whose principal work was the *Arithmetica*.[193] To the same century must be referred yet another remarkable mathema-

---

192 Th. Mommsen. *Römische Geschichte*, Vol. V. (1909 ed.), p. 252. On Plutarch as a biographer see W. Mollendorf. *Reden und Vorträge*, II, 247.

193 *Diophanti Alexandrini opera omnia cum graecis commentariis* ed. Paulus Tannery, Vols. I & II, Lipsiae 1893-5.

tician, Pappus, from the Ptolemaid. From Egypt, too, came
the famous mathematician, astronomer and geographer Claudius Ptolemaeus (Ptolemy) (213-273 AD) who inspired Colum-
bus to undertake his voyages in search of the "Indies".[194] Opposed as they were to the spirit of superstition and magic
which flooded the Greek world from the first century AD, the
scientific traditions of the Museum at Alexandria had not
yet been wiped out. The Roman imperial government granted exemption from taxes and relief from all other public
service to doctors and teachers and it was perhaps on this
account that the Empire produced so many medical men
who in the cause of humanity and of their nation spent
freely on public philanthropic institutions, especially in Asia
Minor. In addition, we have medical scholars and writers
of this same period, the most famous of all being Galen (129-
199 AD) of Pergamon, a true medical philosopher and a
scholar of encyclopaedic learning, who laid the foundations
of further progress in anatomy and philosophy by his experiments on animals. He wrote a large number of works
but unfortunately lost many of his manuscripts in a fire in
Rome.

Another medical scholar from Pergamon, of later date and
lesser stature, was Orivasius, the counsellor of the Emperor
Julian. Contemporary with Galen were the physician Aretaeus
of Cappadocia and Marcellus of Sidea in Pamphylia. Asia
also gave to the world at a latter period (sixth century) the
physicians Aetius of Amida in Syria and Alexander of Tralles
who, with Paul of Aegina (seventh century), may be considered
the three latest of the important medical figures of antiquity.

The traditions of literary criticism, too, continued unbroken,
since Atticism at least required study of the ancient writers
and the aid of scientific literary study was consequently in
demand. Herodian of Alexandria was a famous grammarian
in the time of Marcus Aurelius and the author of a work on
prosody. Herodian's father, Apollonius, known as "the Difficult," was likewise a grammarian of note and his works were
copied by the Romans, particularly by the grammarian Pris-
cian. A part of the book of Apollonius on syntax has been

preserved.

Harpocratian was another Alexandrian, and Polydeuces from Naucratis. Dionysius the Younger came from Halicarnassus and Phrynichus from Bithynia. All these were writers of the second century.

The famous lexicographer Hesychius, who lived probably in the fifth century AD, was likewise from Alexandria: his dictionary is of particular value in that it contains words unknown from other sources, which are, however, often found in dialects of modern Greek.

In the Christian era adherents of the ancient philosophical systems were still to be found, in some cases great and original minds. The slave Epictetus from Hierapolis in Phrygia attained the stature of a great Stoic philosopher and a life worthy of Socrates. The opinions and observations of Epictetus were recorded, as those of Socrates were by Xenophon, by a disciple of his from Nicomedia in Bithynia, Flavius Arrianus (95-175 AD) in the second century. The power and vigor of the Stoic philosophy are evident from the fact that an emperor like Marcus Aurelius (161-169), the noblest of the Romans, wrote his *Reflections* in Greek.

Historians and Geographers

Some attention is claimed by the long succession of historians which continues into the Christian era. Among the first should be noted the two Jewish historians of the first century, Philo (10 BC - 50 AD) and Josephus (37 - 63 AD) who served his country against the Romans but subsequently remained as a prisoner of war at Rome and wrote his *Jewish Antiquities* and his work *On the Jewish War*. The same Arrianus (Arrian) mentioned above wrote an *Alexander's Expedition* in imitation of Xenophon's *Anabasis*. The most important Greek historian of the imperial age was, however, Dio Cassius Cocceianus (155-235 AD) of Nicaea in Bythynia, who was a senior official in the Roman service and wrote on Roman history as an eye-witness and on first-hand information. After Tacitus Rome produced no historian who could rank with Dio Cassius, since the irresponsible Suetonius can hardly be compared with him.

In the second century the Alexandrian Appian (d. 160

AD) also wrote a "Roman History" in which he examined the subjugation of the East.

In the fourth century the Greek Ammianus Marcellinus, from Antioch, the contemporary and admirer of Julian, wrote in Latin a Roman History of which there survives only the section from Constantine to the death of Valens.

The fanatical pagan Eunapius of Sardis in Lydia (345-420 AD) wrote a history of the years 270-404, in continuation of the history of Dexippus, as well as lives of the Sophists.

Olympiodorus, of the Egyptian Thebes, wrote a chronicle of the years 409-425. Zosimus, in the fifth century, wrote a history from Augustus down to Theodosius II; he was a zealous adherent of the old religion.

In the reign of Theodosius the sophist Priscus, from Panion in Thrace, wrote a Byzantine history, that is to say a history of the city of Byzantium, a work continued by Malchus, of Philadelphia in Palestine, who likewise wrote a work entitled *Byzantiaca*. The last of the pagan historians was the sixth century Hesychius Illustris of Miletus.

Next, mention must be made of the writers of memoirs and of works on travel. Of these the most important is Pausanias, probably a native of Lydia, who in the second century wrote a *Tour of Greece*, the first book to inculde purely archaeological and religious information.

The geographer Strabo (63 BC - 19 AD) was born at Amasea in Pontus of a family of Cretan origin. Claudius Aelianus was born near Rome and is therefore called a Roman, but he wrote his *Historical Medley* (Ποικίλη Ἱστορία) in Greek. Athenaeus, of Naucratis in Egypt, was the author of the *Philosophers at Dinner* (Δειπνοσοφισταὶ)

Sophists and Poets

The famous treatise *On the Sublime* was probably composed in the first century AD; it has been attributed to Longinus of Emesa, a fellow-disciple of Plotinus, who was killed after the capture and sack of Palmyra by the Romans. In the second century we encounter a revival of Greek letters. In addition to the historians named above—Arrian, Dio Cassius, Appian, the learned Plutarch and the physician Galen — mention must be made of famous sophists and orators, like Aelius Aristides,

Dio Chrysostom and others, who had Origen and Clement
as their contemporaries. At this same period the Roman West
was marked by cultural decline.

The third century is characterized by the Neoplatonic philoso-
ophy and by religous literature. In a sense it forms a contrast
to the third century BC which was conspicious, above all for
the advancement of science.

Aelius Aristides (117-189 AD was born at Adrianou Therae
(the modern Balikesir) and wrote in an exaggerated style,
very much in the manner of "Asian flamboyance." The most
celebrated of the new Sophists was from Greece, the Herodes
Atticus already named above. Lucian(120 - 180 A.D.) of
Samosata in Syria (now Samsat) was a restless spirit, typically
Greco-Syrian in his mental pliability, who frequently changed
his views, his outlook and his profession. He wrote a variety
of essays, marked by sarcasm and a bitter irony.

Dio Chrysostom was born at Prusa in Bithynia in the first
century AD. He travelled widely and his "Discourses" are
of value for the information they give on Greek civilization
at that time.

From the fourth century on we find famous sophists and
orators or teachers of rhetoric. The most famous of all is the
Neoplatonist Libanius (314—393) of Antioch, who was the
teacher of St. John Chrysostom. The humane culture and
wisdom of Libanius made him an object of reverence to pagans
and Christians alike. His humanitarian outlook emerges at
many points in his writings. In his discourse *On Patronage*
(XLVII in Vol. III, p. 404 in Foerster's edition) he speaks of
the cruelties inflicted on the poor by taxgatherers, soldiers and
others in positions of power and of their being forced to
seek the protection of some rich man. In his Twenty-Ninth
Discourse, Section 13, he writes of himself: "Who does not
know that whenever I walk through the city I never pass
anyone I see weeping, but stop in distress and seek out the
wrongdoer. If I catch him, I make him pay the penalty; if
I cannot, it grieves my heart . . . I am well able not to exact
retribution from those who have made bold against myself
but if anyone else is in trouble, I cannot bear it."

Himerius of Prusa (310—386), a pupil of the Neoplatonist
Proairesius and son-in-law of the priest Nicagoras, was an ini-
tiate of the mysteries of Mithras. He wrote eighty discourses,

sixty of which were known to Photius. One interesting observation of his may be recorded: "The Greeks formerly conquered the world by force of arms: now they conquer by the excellence of their rulers."

Themisticus of Paphlagonia (317 - 388) was acceptable to the Christians and addressed to Theodosius I his work, "*Which is the most royal of the virtues?*" He was an advocate of religious tolerance. The position of distinction which he held (he was a Senator and Court Counsellor) transformed him from a teacher of philosophy into an orator.

The last pagan oratory made its appearance in the last place one would have dreamed of, namely at Gaza in Palestine,[195] on the frontiers of Arabia. The chief sophists of Gaza were Procopius, Aeneas, Zacharias, the orator Choricius, who lived in the reigns of Justin and Justinian, and others beside.

The art of rhetoric outlived Greek philosophy and science and even had an influence on Christian literature. Of all Greek literary forms rhetoric lived longest and had the widest effect. The so-called "literature of love" (ἐρωτικοὶ λόγοι), or novel, also came under the influence of rhetoric. It was a new form of writing which produced no great work in the earlier periods of its existence but was later to have a world-wide significance and to give birth, in modern times, to masterpieces in greater numbers than any other form of literature.

Chariton of Aphrodisias, in Caria, wrote, probably in the first or second and not in the fifth century,[196] the oldest novel which had been preserved. *The tale of Chaereas and Callirhoe*, in seven books. In imitation of him, Xenophon of Ephesus later wrote *The Ephesian Tale of Anthea and Habrocome*, in five books, and Heliodorus, of Emesa in Syria (to be distinguished

195 The Arab city of Gaza may be described as a Greek miracle, since Greek poetry, rhetoric and philosophy were so highly cultivated there. "The city of Gaza was devoted to the arts and had brought the art of letters to a high pitch of perfection." See E. Legier, "Essia de biographie d'Enée de Gaza" in *Oriens Christiana*, VII (1907), p. 349; P. Friedländed. *Spätantike Gemäldezyklus in Gaza. A Portrait of Procopius of Gaza*. P. Friedrich. *Johannes von Gaza und Paulus Silentiarius*, 1912. *Chorici Gazaei opera* ed. R. Foerster & E. Richtsteig, 1929. In an encomium on Marcian, Bishop of Gaza, it is said: "The memory of those who have lived holy lives is a great training for the practice of virtue."

196 Christ-Schmid-Stählin. *Geschichte der Griechischen Literatur*, Vol. II. 2 (1924), p. 808.

from the bishop of Tricca of the same name),[197] wrote, probably in the third century, *The Tale of Theagenes and Chariclea or Aethiopica*, the most widely read of these romances. It was probably also in the third century that Longus wrote his pastoral romance *The Tale of Daphnis and Chloe* which Goethe praised so highly. Finally, in the fifth century Achilles Tatius, of Alexandria, wrote the last of the ancient romances, *The Tale of Leucippe and Cleitophon.*

A great expansion of didactic poetry took place and gave birth to a few works of merit. The leader of those writing in the older style was Aratus, from soli in Cilicia, with his *Phenomena*. Babrius, who may have been a Roman, wrote tales in Greek, in the choliambic or mythiambic metre. Oppian, a Cilician, dedicated to Marcus Aurelius his poem on fishing, the *Halieutica*. Yet another author composed an Orphic poem on the magical power of stones, entitled the *Lithica*." Nonnus from Panopolis in Egypt wrote the *Dionysiaca*, a mythological poem about Dionysus. Nonnus later became a Christian and turned St. John's Gospel into verse. He was succeeded by other mythological poets: Tryphiodorus wrote on the sack of Troy, Coluthus, a native of Lycopolis in Egypt, on the rape of Helen. Musaeus, too, shows the influence of Nonnus in his love poem, *The Tale of Hero and Leander*, which was the most charming romance of antiquity. A contemporary of Nonnus was the Alexandrian Greek Claudian who began writing mythological poems but later wrote in Latin in the West and celebrated the deeds of Stilicho at the court of Honorius, the successor of Theodosius.

The *epigram* is a form of poetry which has been cultivated in Greek for thousands of years, and Greek epigrams have been written from the days of Simonides to our own. In the period of which we are speaking masterpieces in this form were written by many of the Asian poets.

The Neopythagoreans and Neoplationists

Little by little the old philosophic systems felt the religious influence of the East and Egypt and were adapted to new spiritual needs; and it was this way that the systems of the

---

[197] Christ-Schmid-Stählin. *op. cit.*, p. 820.

Neopythagoreans and the Neoplatonists came into being. The most eminent of the Neopythagoreans was Apollonius of Tyana, [198] whose life and work was described in the third century AD by Flavius Philostratus of Lemnos.[199] Apollonius led an ascetic life after the manner of Pythagoras and abstained from meat. He made long journeys into Asia as far as Ctesiphon, teaching his doctrine by his own personal example.[200] Orphic and oriental ideas combined in the teaching of the Neopythagoreans, who sought communion with God.

The teaching of the founder of the Neoplatonic philosophy, the Egyptian Ammonius (175-242 AD)[201] was systematized and supplemented by Plotinus (204-269) of Lycopolis in Egypt, who considered himself a disciple of Plato rather than of Ammonius. He was a man of temperate mind, wholly dedicated to his creed, an ascetic by nature and a person of charm. In Rome, where he lived, he was held in high regard by, among others, the Emperor Gallienus, whom he besought to found a city, Platonopolis, in Plato's honour.[202] Plotinus's life was written by his disciple Porphyrius who relates a variety of stories, typical of the confidence which men showed him (*Life of Plotinus*, IV, 5): ". . . And many men and women of

198 Philostratus IV. 1. "Apollonius was a native of Tyana, a Greek city among a population of Cappadocians."

199 Th. Hopfner. "Apollonios von Tyana und Philostratos," in *Seminarium Kondakovianum*, Vol. IV (1931), p. 134 ff.

200 When he visited the city of Aspendus in Pamphylia, the inhabitants were living only on chickpeas, "since the ruling classes had shut away the corn in order that it might be exported from the country." The people had become infuriated and were preparing to burn the "cornchandlers" when Apollonius stepped in and induced the black marketeers of Aspendus to dispose of the corn in the local market. (Philostratus XV). Apollonius, in his philosophy, held that the soul was immortal.

201 Another disciple of Ammonius was, according to Eunapius, (*Lives of the Philosophers and Sophists*, Didot, p. 454) the "Most Divine" and "Marvellous" Plutarch.

202 Plotiuns. *Life*, Ch. 12 : The Emperor Gallienus and his wife Solonina honoured and revered Plotinus. And he, availing himself of their friendship, asked for the restoration of a certain city of philosophers, which was said to have existed in Campania but was subsequently ruined, and for the grant of the surrounding country to the city on its resettlement. Those who were to populate it should observe Plato's laws and it should have the name of Platonopolis; and Plotinus himself undertook to repair there with the rest."

the noblest families (of Rome), when they were at the point of death, took their children, both boys and girls, and entrusted them to him, with the rest of their possessions, as to a holy and revered guardian."

Plotinus exercised, perhaps, a greater influence through his ascetic life than through his teachings.[203] His system of philosophy interests us here mainly in its practical aspect, according to which man enters into communication with the Supreme Being by means of ecstasy. His philosophy, therefore, was among those which aimed at the communion with the divine which was so ardently desired in Hellenic and Roman times, but despite its asceticism it was opposed to Gnosticism which aimed still higher, at deliverance from the body and a new life.[204] In this respect, the Neoplatonism of Plotinus and his successors, which was so greatly influenced by the mysteries and by the magical elements of Eastern religion, was more akin to the Christianity against which it fought than to the ancient world which it was defending.

Among the disciples of Plotinus was Malchus of Tyre (233-303 AD), nicknamed Porphyrius by the teacher Longinus. He was not in agreement with Plotinus on all points but agreed with him wholly as regards communion with the divine through ecstasy. Porphyrius attacked Christianity, and as an ascetic, he also wrote against the eating of meat.

Iamblichus, the disciple of Porphyrius (d. 330 AD) was a Syrian from the Syrian Chalcis, and this explains how it was that Neoplatonic philosophy gradually drew away from Plato and drew steadily closer to the religions of Egypt and the East. Iamblichus was a theologian rather than a philosopher and believed in magic and in a variety of mystic cults.

With Proclus (410-485 AD), a native of Xanthus in Lycia, Athens became the headquarters of the Neoplatonists. Proclus too was beloved as a god-fearing, virtuous and learned man. The return to Athens, however, could not divorce him from the mysticism of the East: he wrote among other works

203 According to Eunapius (op. cit., 46), Plotinus "owing to the unworldliness of his mind and his oracular manner and the obscurity of his words appeared heavy and abstruse."

204 J. Geffeken. Der Ausgang des griechisch-römischen Heidentums, 1920, p. 39 ff.

a hymn to the Sun, to whom he prayed three times a day. When Asclepigenia, the daughter of the Neoplatonist Plutarch, was ill, Proclus undertook to cure her by prayers to Aesculapius.[205]

The Neoplatonist Hypatia, the daughter of the mathematician Theon, taught at Alexandria: among her pupils was Synesius who later became a convert to Christianity. In 415 AD Hypatia was murdered by Christian fanatics as an enemy to their religion.

The last of the Neoplatonists, Simplicius, was less of a mystic, but the closing of the School at Athens (529 AD) under the economic pressure of Justinian could not greatly injure the Neoplatonic philosophy, which contained no further seeds of life and development.

Christian Literature

We have mentioned a number of names from the various branches of literature mainly in order to show from which cities of Asia and Egypt their exponents came and, consequently, the expansion of Greek culture. This expansion is also illustrated by the earliest Christian literature which was chiefly the work of Greeks in Egypt and Asia. The apologists, catechists, historians and poets of Christianity of the first centuries were nearly all Greeks or were under Greek influence.

The fact that the *Gospels* and the *Acts of the Apostles* were written in Greek is already a proof of the significance of the Greek language and Greek letters. Early Christianity, of course, owed its expansion to its humanitarian activity; it was continuously active, it was not concerned with abstract debate and it had no literary needs. But from the second century on, as soon as it had spread far enough afield, it came

---

[205] Marinus Neapolitanus. *Proclus, or On Happiness*, Ch. XXVI, *Ibid.* XVII: "If any of his friends fell ill, he (Proclus) first entreated the gods with sacrifices and hymns on his behalf, and then bestowed every attention on the sick man, collecting the physicians and urging them to use their professional skill unsparingly." The same work (Ch. XVIII) also contains the following on mystic ceremonies: "He (Proclus) employed deprecations and sprinklings and other purifying charms, some Orphic and some Chaldean, and each month he went down to the sea without fail (to purify himself)."

into conflict with paganism and Gnosticism and found it necessary to fight them and to rebut the accusations levelled at the Christian religion. From the second century, therefore, the first great Christian writers began to appear at Alexandria, initially, with its literary traditions. After the former Stoic Pantaenus and after Clement, the most eminent figure is that of Origen (185-254 AD), the son of the teacher and martyr Leonidas. Origen was the first to systematize, under the influence of Platonic philosophy, Christian theology up to his time. He was put to the torture under Decius and died at Tyre. His immense learning and his martyrdom made him greatly admired but his theology later aroused opposition. Nevertheless, Origen remains the first great Christian writer and one of the greatest the Church has produced.[206]

Himself a disciple of Ammonius, Origen became in his turn a renowned teacher with a crowd of pupils, "who attended his school one after another from dawn to evening." (Eusebius *History*, VI, 15).

Pamphilus, who was the master of Eusebius, was an admirer and defender of Origen and founded, in traditional style, a library of some 3000 volumes in the Palestinian Caesarea: he was martyred in 309 AD.

Another of Origen's pupils, St. Gregory the Wonderworker (213-270 AD), who came from Neocaesarea (now Niksar) is of special importance for his transmission of Christianity to the interior of Asia Minor and Armenia and for his foundation of the Cappadocian Church.

Eusebius, who was called "the son of Pamphilus" after his beloved master, was the founder of Church history as a special branch of historical literature, his own work going as far as 323 AD. His example was followed by Socrates, of Constantinople (380); Sozomen, from the environs of Gaza; the Cappadocian Philotorgius (358); Theodoret, bishop of Cyrrus in Syria (393-458); Gelasius of Cyzicus; and Evagrius, also a Syrian, from Epiphanea (536-600). The large number of ecclesiastical historians shows the importance attached at this time to the Christian Church.

The cessation of the persecutions from the time of Con-

206 Christopher Dawson in *The Making of Europe* considers that Origen was the greatest thinker of the Greek world.

stantine gave the Church free scope for development. We have seen that the Alexandrian Greek, Athanasius, (300-373 AD) distinguished himself at the First Ecumenical Council in 325. After becoming Patriarch, he submitted without hesitation to banishment and persecution if only his views might prevail. But he also achieved distinction as a writer,[207] and through his *Life of St. Antony*, written after the ancient model of the biographies of Pythagoras and Plotinus, he imposed the ascetic standards of St. Antony and his follow-ers.[208]

The fourth century marked in fact the end of the ancient world and the beginning of the Christian Middle Ages. In this transitional period Christian men of learning established relations with the pagan teachers and these relations seem to have been extremely fruitful. Thus, two of the greatest Fathers of the Church, Basil the Great (331-379) and Gregory Nazianzene (330-390), studied at Athens with great advantage. Both came from Cappadocia, together with Basil's brothers, Gregory, Bishop of Nyssa (d. 395). St. Basil himself, who was Bishop of Caesarea in Cappadocia from 370 AD, showed great organising ability: he introduced monastic life,[209] but made it at the same time less severe, since he combined it with letters, handwork and philanthropic activity: he founded the "Basilead," the first great philanthrop establishment, where orphans could obtain not only relief but education. His pugnacious character drove him to the defense of the Church against Arianism, and he became renowned as a fiery writer, whose opinions the Church has always held in reverence.

Besides encouraging the humanitarian spirit and combating excessive wealth [210] and luxury, Basil the Great enjoined upon Christians by his authority the reading of the ancient Greek

207 H. Opitz began a fine edition of the work of Athanasius in 1934, but his death in the Second World War unfortunately prevented its completion..

208 M. Constantinides. "The life and community of the holy Father Antony by Athanasius," (in Greek) in *Ekklesiastikos Pharos*, Vol. XXXII (1933) p. 582 and Vol. XXXIII, p. 115.

209"Basil toured the cities of the Black Sea region and founded many monastic settlements there." (Sozomen, *Ecclesiastical History*, VI, 17, 4).

210 See the relevant passages in D. Stephanides. *Social Economics in their Historical Development* (in Greek), Vol I. (1948), p. 255 ff.

authors. In his famous essay *How to profit by Greek literature* (Chaps. IV and V), he writes, "As in picking roses off the
tree, we avoid the thorns, so in literature of this kind (i.e.
Greek literature) we shall guard against what is harmful,
while gathering all that is profitable." And about Homer he
writes: "As I heard a man say who was skilled in penetrating
a poet's thought, the whole of Homer's poetry is a praise of
virtue and everything in him tends to this end . . ." St. Basil's
works have been published in Migne's *Patrologia Graeca*,[211]
vols. XXIX to XXXII.

Gregory Nazianzene, the son of Bishop Gregory of Nazianzus
in Cappadocia and the brother of Caesarius, the Emperor
Julian's physician, had not Basil's pugnacious character nor
his powers of organization, but he was a man of greater mental
resources and showed his wealth of intellect in his Church
hymns (he was the founder of ecclesiastical poetry) and in his
other poems, among which are those which contain his auto-
biography, *On himself* and the *Lament for his spiritual
sufferings.* His great reputation carried him to the patriarchal
throne of Constantinople in 380, where, however, he held of-
fice for a short time only, since he had not the spirit needed
to combat the various factions opposing him. After retiring
from the Patriarchate he devoted himself to study and wrote
a large number of works which are prized both for their literary and for their historical value. It was he who termed
Athanasius, the Patriarch of Alexandria, the Great and said
of him (Migne *PG* 35, 1081): "In prising Athanasius, I shall
be praising virtue herself." Of St. Cyprian (*ibid.*, 1176) he
says: "This is he who was once a great name in Carthage,

---

[211] Of Basil's philanthropic work Gregory Nazianzene writes, in his *Funeral
Discourse on Bishop Basil* (Chap. 34 in Boulanger's edition): "His succour
to the needy was in most cases spiritual, but in not a few material: he
fed the poor, entertained strangers, gave dowries to young girls . . ." And
further on (Chap. 63) he writes of the "Basilead." "Go a little way out
of the town (i.e. Caesarea) and see the new city, the treasure-house of
piety, the common treasure of those that possess it, which makes them to
abound in wealth . . ." Basil's forcefulness and spirit appear admirably
in the answer he returned to the Arian governor Modestus who tried to
threaten him: "Fire and sword and wild beasts and claws tearing the
flesh are an indulgence rather than a terror. Therefore, insult, threaten,
do anything you will, revel in your authority. Let the emperor himself
hear this, that you will never persuade us to treat with impiety, though you
threaten greater hardships still." This famous reply is enough in itself
to explain Basil's great authority among Christians.

and whose name is now great throughout the world." To the
governor Sophronius he writes (*ibid.*, 37, 77) : "To honour
one's mother is a sacred duty, but each of us has a different
mother: our common mother is our country." He calls the
rhetor Themistius a great man and "a king of words" (*ibid.*,
37, 60 and 80). In his will he left his estate "to the Catholic
Church of Nazianzus for the service of the poor who are
under the said Church," [212] which was to appoint three almon-
ers (*ibid.*, 37, 389).

One of the most attractive figures of the Church was Synesius (370-412), who was among the last of the Greeks of
Cyrene. Synesius was a disciple of the Neoplatonic philosopher
Hypatia; he defended his country gallantly against the incursions of the native Africans and the maladministration of
the imperial officials. He became a Christian and a bishop at
the entreaty of his compatriots in order that he might be
better able to help his country. His adherence to Christianity
was therefore not without inner reservations. In his writings
he used the Doric dialect of his homeland. He composed
hymns (including even one to Nemesis) and other poems,
and generally speaking, this late-enlightened Christian should
rather be considered as the last champion of Greek culture
in Africa.

The greatest of all the Fathers of the Church was the
Antiochene John Chrysostom (344-407 AD) a pupil of the celebrated Libanius and of Theodore, Bishop of Mopsuestia in
Cilicia. His fame as an orator and his moral force raised
Chrysostom from the provinces to the Patriarch's throne at
Constantinople (398-404) where he took up the struggle
against the corrupt nobility that led to his banishment and
death. Chrysostom was marked by his love for the suffering
people and his passion for the moral elevation of mankind,
and in his fight for these ideals he was indomitable. He was,
at the same time, the greatest orator of the Church, inasmuch
as he expressed his feelings and views with sincerity and

---

212 On Gregory Nazianzene see D. Balanos. *Patrologia*, 1930, p. 304 (in
Greek) ; E. Fleury. *Hellénisme et Christianisme. St Grégoire de Nazianze
et son temps*, 1. 30; P. Gallay. *La Vie de Saint Grégoire de Nazianze*, 1943.
The works of Gregory Nazianzene have been published in Migne's *Patrologia Graeca*, 35-37.

strength and in the plain Greek of his time. An immense number of writings — speeches, sermons, letters, etc. — are attributed to him, but they include some which are spurious.

Non-Greek Literatures

It is typical of the time that Greek Christian culture should have helped to form new foreign literatures, Aramaic, Coptic, Armenian, and later Slavonic. Neither the Egyptians nor the Syrians nor the Armenians had created literatures of their own in the pre-Christian era, although they had been in contact with the Greeks for centuries. But the need to transmit the Christian religion, with its catechism, its liturgy and other literature gave rise to translations from the Greek and into Greek and to the composition of works in the vernacular. As the official language of Syria and Palestine in the time of the Achaemenids and later, Aramaic was of course employed in inscriptions, but these hardly constitute a literature. From 200 AD onwards the Aramic dialect of Edessa in Syria began to be used increasingly in translations of the Gospels but also in poems and other original work.[213] Later on, in the fourth century AD, Syrian writers like Ephraim the Syrian appear, whose works were translated into Greek.

The Egyptians, too, after receiving Christianity, created a new alphabet on the Greek model and began to translate the Gospels and other Christian works into the vernacular of the time, namely Coptic. Subsequently the Christian Copts developed a feeling of antagonism towards the Romans and the Greeks and we see this opposition and the feeling of compassion for the Egyptian people in the work of the first founder of monasteries in Egypt, Pachomius (318 AD), and above all in Shenoute. According to Leipoldt Shenoute is of no importance at all in general history, but for the Copts he is of supreme importance since he gave them a national Church and a national literature and worked for the relief of his people. It was in fact due to the existence of a Coptic national literature that after the Arab deluge Coptic Christians sur-

213 See T. Nöldeke. "Die aramäische Literatur in Hinneberg," *Die Kultur der Gegenwart* 1. VII (1906), pp. 103, 104, ff.

vived in Egypt, whereas they did not survive in Africa, which had used Latin in the Church.

In the fourth century the Goths received Christianity, chiefly in the form of Arianism, through the agency of Ulfilas (311-382), a native of Asia Minor, who compiled the first German and Gothic alphabet out of Greek and old runic elements and translated the scriptures into Old German and Gothic.

CHAPTER VIII

DIOCLETIAN AND CONSTANTINE

The Chaos of the Third Century

The third century could hardly fail to produce economic stagnation and political chaos throughout the Roman world, since besides the German tribal invasions there took place internally the great social upheaval which has already been described. To the causes of political and economic confusion must be added the fact that from 193 AD, that is to say from the time of Pertinax, up to Diocletian's accession in 284 as many as fifty emperors were proclaimed after successful insurrections, and with the exception of Septimius Severus (193-211), Alexander Severus (222-235) and Aurelian (270-275), few were equal to their opportunities. One man, for example, Elagabalus, a priest of the Sun from Emesa in Syria, became emperor merely because he bore a resemblance to Caracalla and persuaded the army that he was his son. Another emperor, Philip, (244-249) was an Arab, and Maximin the Thracian was the offspring of a German father and an Alan mother.[214] The majority of the third century emperors were Illyrian.

All these disturbances, which were due to the continual changes on the throne, helped to produce chaos and decline; but even apart from this, the crushing pressure of the Empire on so many people was fatally bound to bring its own revenge. The fortification of the interminable frontiers by the *Limes* of Hadrian had proved powerless to check indefinitely the attacks and invasions of so many neighboring, highly warlike nations, as for instance the Germans, hostile Aurelian was obliged to protect even Rome itself with a strong wall.

Other causes too contributed to the confusion. From the East there came not only the worship of Mithras but the

214 K. Pfister. *Der Untergang der antiken Welt*, 1941, p. 164.

cults of other deities as well and these sapped the old religious beliefs of the Romans. The persecutions of Christianity did not check the spread of its humanitarian ideas but, on the contrary, strengthened it.

These military and civil disturbances practically brought to a standstill all commercial exchange and the collection of taxes and caused a fall in the value of the currency. The chaos of the third century was the fatal consequence of the extension of the Roman conquests and the retribution for their oppression of so many conquered peoples. The turning-point between the Roman and the medieval worlds must be located in the age of Diocletian and Constantine.

Diocletian gave Rome absolute monarchy and his work was completed by Constantine. It is sometimes difficult to distinguish between the legislation and the administration of these two emperors. Aurelian (270-275) had already laid the foundations of absolutism, since he had aimed, among other things, at religious unification (the cult of Helios-Mithras), he had reinforced the imperial power not only by practical measures but, after the example of the Sassanids, by heightening its external brilliance (the adoption of the purple and of the imperial diadem), and it was he who had enforced the rule of heredity in trades and professions. He styled himself divine (*deus et dominus*) and united the worship of the emperor and the worship of God.

Diocletian [215] was an Illyrian from Dalmatia and was proclaimed Augustus by the army in 284 at Nicomedia, where he had built a palace and habitually resided. He was the first emperor who preferred the East to the West, perhaps because he felt a dislike for Rome with its reactionary Senate, to which, however, he continued to leave its conventional dignitaries and the care of the city of Rome. But the autocracy at which Diocletian was aiming could not be combined with the authority of the Roman senate. At Nicomedia this authority could not be felt. It was significant that Diocletian kept as his chief minister the experienced politician Aristobulus, who was

---

[215] E. Stein. *Geschichte des spätrömischen Reiches*, Vol. I. (1928), p. 94 ff. Diocletian originally bore the Greek name Diocles: he was an indefatigable planner who pursued his plans inflexibly. See Pfister, *op. cit.*, p. 199.

probably a Greek and was in consequence very well suited
to deal with the East.

The Bacaudae

At the beginning of Diocletian's reign many rebellions
took place, and among these special attention is due to the
revolt of the Gallic land-workers the Bacaudre as Zosimus
calls them, using the Celtic name by which they have ever
since been known to history. In Gaul, as elsewhere in the
Roman Empire, huge estates had been formed, the development of which Rome had reinforced by entrusting to the big
landowners the collection of the taxes and of certain legal
and administrative dues. The landowners, in their turn, had
lost no time in unloading the taxes upon their tenants and
on the small farmers, who obtained no protection from Rome.
Many were then forced to seek the patronage of the landlords
in very much the same way as had happened at Rome in
earlier times when the plebians had turned themselves into
clientes under patrician patronage. Thus by its miserable
economic mismanagement Rome delivered its agricultural populations to the mercy of the landlords. It is understandable
that the spirited country folk of Gaul felt unable to accept in
perpetuity and on arbitrary terms the patronage of the landowners and that a labourers' revolt broke out in consequence,
just as that other peasant revolt known as the Jacquerie broke
out in France towards the end of the Middle Ages. This revolt
of the Bacaudae was put down with difficulty by Diocletian
through the agency of the Illyrian general Maximian from
Pannonia.

Joint Rulers

These frequent and stubborn revolts forced the autocratic
Diocletian to seek the help of associates whom he could en-
deavor to attach to himself by marriage ties in the hope
that by kinship and adoption he might prevent clashes
between them. He therefore called in Maximian, first as an
ally and as Caesar, and later as Augustus. He himself took
the further title of *Jovius*, while giving Maximian that of

Herculius: this distinction of titles demonstrated Diocletian's paternal relation, as in some sort the Jupiter to Maximian's Hercules. Maximian usually resided at Milan, not in Rome, and had to deal with the Germanic invasion of the Alamanni and the Franks, while Diocletian retained the legislative power and the guardianship of the Danube frontier which was constantly attacked by Sarmatians and Goths.

Maximian's docility caused Diocletian to overrate the system of joint rulers and, in 283, to nominate two more Illyrians as Caesars, the former herdsman Galerius from Sardica (the modern Sofia) and Constantius Chlorus from Naissus (now Nish in Serbia), both of whom he attached to him by marriage. Constantius took to wife Theodora, a daughter-in-law of Maximian, and Galerius Diocletian's daughter. Galerius remained with Diocletian in the East, Constantius with Maximian in the West.

Administration and Economics

Diocletian was not content with the partnership of four; he altered the administrative and in part the economic system. He completed his organization of a salaried government service, in order that he might not have to fear the Senate or powerful provincial governors. To prevent the growth of powerful subordinates he divided the Empire into twelve dioceses, which in turn were subdivided into some hundred eparchies. He had to separate the political administration entirely from the military, a policy later carried to its conclusion by Constantine. He devoted particular attention to the frontiers and their fortification; in these areas military and civil government were both still concentrated in one hand. And for the sake of frontier defense he greatly increased his army, to some 500,000 men.

The increasing of the army, however, led inevitably to an increase in expenditure, and Diocletian was hard put to it to find the money required in an age of the most fearful economic crisis, which called for an abatement rather than an increase in taxation. Once again, the system of taxation (poll tax, cattle tax and the rest) weighed most heavily on the agricultural population. When later Galerius attempted to make the inhabitants of the towns pay these taxes, Rome, which now lay apart from the centre of things, rebelled and in 306 proclaimed its own Augustus, Maxentius, Maximian's son, who favoured the poorer classes.

Finding himself in an economic impasse, Diocletian redoubled and made still more severe the various measures of taxation and compulsion employed by the state. The rural taxation mentioned above threw the agricultural population on the mercy of the landowners whose protection they accordingly sought. The state of affairs which had provoked the rising of the Gallic peasantry some years before had not been remedied in any way; on the contrary, it had grown worse. Hitherto the farmer had been personally free but obliged to work the lord's land, but under the new and worse conditions he lost even his freedom[216] and became a serf like the ancient Helot.

The system of compulsion was extended all over the Empire, since no one was in a position to work freely. The soldier's son was obliged to become a soldier himself, the artisan's son an artisan, the official's an official, and so on. Diocletian proceeded to take yet another step in this direction. In 301 he issued his ordinance on controlled prices (edictum de pretiis rerum venalium) which defined the maximum prices in commercial transactions and also the maximum wage.[217] The seller, in particular, was most severely hit by this limitation of prices. The measure in question produced a bad effect on the market, since food supplies were hidden, and Constantine was later compelled to rescind it.

Persecutions

Diocletian was a conservative Roman and his religious conservatism combined with his autocratic conception of government to drive him into religious persecution of the Christians. The initial impulse came in 303 from a fire which broke out at Nicomedia and was attributed to the Christians. It was,

[216] E. Hohl. "Die römische Kaiserzeit," in Propyläen-Weltgeschichte, Vol. I (1931), p. 436.

[217] H. Blumner. Der maximal tarif des Diokletian. 1893.

however, Galerius who insisted strongly on launching the persecutions, although he was the man who was later to be the
first to issue the edict of toleration.

The persecutions followed a different course in different areas.
In the West, for example, Constantius only applied very mildly
the ordinances which gave effect to them. In Nicomedia, however, and elsewhere in the East there were massacres of Christians, including bishops, in thousands. At the same time the
Christians suffered other forms of persecution as well. They
lost their military and civil positions and their civil rights.
The liberation of Christian slaves was forbidden, churches and
Christian writings were destroyed and finally, the compulsory
practice of pagan worship was imposed. These measures of
compulsion against the Christians strengthened the Church
further and had consequently to be annulled very soon after.

It should be noted that at the very time when Diocletian
was persecuting the Christians, the first national Christian
Church was being founded in the East. After the victory of
Galerius over the Persians in 297, Tiridates, the friend of
the Romans, was recognized as independent and sovereign king
of Armenia. He adopted Christianity, which had been introduced into his country by Gregory the Illuminator, and he
allowed it to be practiced freely in his kingdom. In fact, the
young King Tiridates had a better insight into the real state
of affairs than Diocletian, who was so deeply sunk in preju-
dice.

Diocletian extended his arbitrary measures as far as to
abolish the right of the city of Alexandria to mint Greek
coins. Constantine later completed this process by doing away
with every vestige of municipal autonomy in the Greek cities.
The conservative Diocletian had no hesitation in adopting
the rich and austere ceremonial of the Sassanid court in order
to endow his own autocracy with some outward glamour. He

218 According to Joannes Lydus (περὶ ἀρχῶν) I, 4) Diocletian "was the
first to wear a crown of precious stones on his head and to wear 'mosaic
shoes' and to show a tendency to play the monarch, or if truth be told, the
tyrant." But from the east came not only the luxury of outward appearance but also the employment of eunuchs and the mutilations which were
such a blot upon Byzantium.

enforced the "adoration" of the Emperor on bended knee and the ruler rarely showed himself to his subjects.[218]

None of the compulsory legislation with which Diocletian attempted to save the Roman world produced satisfactory results. It was perhaps this fact which caused him to abdicate in 305 and to withdraw to his palace at Salona (Split) in Dalmatia, from which for a few more years, until 316, he followed the execution of many absolutist measures by Constantine, but also the radical reversal of his own general policy in the matter of the persecutions. Maximian, too, followed Diocletian into retirement in the same year.

Constantine the Great

Constantine[219] was born, probably about the year 285, at Naissus, the modern Nish, not of the lawful wife of Constantius, Theodora, but of his mistress, Helena. Constantine was greatly devoted to his mother, even to the point of listening to her malicious insinuations and he named the city of Drepanum in Bithynia (which was reputedly her birthplace) Helenopolis in her honour.

We possess little information on Constantine's youth. He distinguished himself in battle at an early age and it was on this account that Constantius trained him, and not one of his legitimate sons, as his successor. In 305 the two first Augusti, Maximian and Diocletian, abdicated and the two Caesars, Galerius and Constantius, were proclaimed Augusti. In 306 Constantius died at York in Britian (where Septimius Severus had also ended his life at an earlier date), after his victory over the Pictish invaders. The army, which viewed his son Constantine with favour, at once proclaimed him Augustus, and this supreme dignity had afterwards to be recognized by his fellow-rulers, although sorely against their will. Constantine's marriage with Fausta, the daughter of Maximian and sister of Maxentius, who had similarly been proclaimed Augustus by the army and people at Rome, assisted his own recognition as Augustus. It should be noted that while throughout the term of Constantine's government of Gaul Christians elsewhere were still suffering under the persecutions of Diocle-

---

219 A. Piganiol. *L'Empereur Constantin*, Paris. 1932; I. Palanque. "Constantin." in A. Duff and E. Galy. *Hommes d'Etat*, Vol. I (1936), p. 335. A. Piganiol. *L'empire chrétien*, 1947.

tian, in Gaul they met with moderate and sensible government. Constantine followed his father's policy in regard to the Christians. Later both his mother Helena and his sister Anastasia became converts, a fact which undoubtedly influenced his policy at the time. In the East Galerius recognized as the new Augustus another Illyrian, Licinius. Similarly, the general Maximin was proclaimed Augustus by his army. Thus, there was now a multiple rule of five Augusti and it was perhaps from this moment that Constantine, with his passion for centralization, began to plan the unification of the imperial government. Acknowledging Apollo-Helios as the supreme god (*summus deus*), he struck coins after the older pattern of Aurelian with the inscription *Soli invicto Comiti*, "To the unconquered Sun, the Guide."

The Defeat of Maxentius

After the death of Galerius in 311 new problems and new alliances were created. Constantine came to an understanding with Licinius to whom he agreed to give his sister Constantia [220] in marriage, against Maxentius and Maximin. It is highly probable that from this time on Constantine not only had in view the reversal of Diocletian's arrangement of joint rulers but was already looking ahead to cooperation with the Christians and therefore came to terms all the more easily with Licinius. Constantine carried on unaided the struggle against Maxentius, and with great success. Like another Napoleon he set out with an army of 30,000 men from his capital at Trier in Gaul (*Augusta Treverorum*), crossed the western Alps, occupied north Italy in spite of strong resistance at Verona and made for Rome. Maxentius awaited him irresolutely with an enormous but undisciplined army of 180,000 and met his attack near Rome; he was completely defeated and was killed at the Milvian bridge.

According to Lactantius,[221] the tutor of Crispus, Constantine's son, Constantine dreamed on the eve of this battle that he

---

[220] Constantius and Constantine were favorite names in families with military gifts and traditions.

[221] A. Alföldi and H. Mattingly. *The Conversion of Constantine and Pagan Rome*, 1948, p 16.

should employ the symbol of Christ (the monogram of the Greek letters Chi (X) and Rho (P) on his soldiers' shields and on his own helmet; according to Eusebius he beheld a new vision, the sign of the Cross with the inscription Ἐν τούτῳ νίκα (In this sign conquer). Licinius too announced that he had seen a vision at the time of his battle with Maximin,[222] just as Aurelian had done earlier; it is my own belief that the young Augusti followed Aurelian, even down to the psychological details, as they did also in other more serious respects.

In Rome Constantine was hailed as a liberator, especially among the richest of the senators whom Maxentius had persecuted and who enthusiastically proclaimed Constantine Augustus. There still remains as a memorial to his victory in 312 the triumphal Arch of Constantine erected at Rome. It is stated on this monument that he defeated Maxentius by Divine grace or inspiration (instinctu divinitatis). There is not a word about Christianity in the inscription.

Constantine recognized at Rome the Christian bishop Hosius who appears to have had some influence upon him. Thenceforward he was more favorable towards Christians but he still dedicated his coinage to Apollo-Helios, Soli Invicto: the Christian banner with XP monogram was placed on the coinage later.

Licinius

Licinius, with perfidious cunning, had not hastened to Constantine's aid in his struggle with Maxentius. In 313 he met

---

222 Piganiol (L'Empereur Constantin, p. 78) writes in regard to these visions and apparitions: "Aurelian's vision in Syria, Constantine's in Gaul, Licinius' in Thrace, all these hallucinations were skillfully exploited by the men who actually experienced them, by politicians and by priests, with the result that it is hard for us today to discern how much in them was credulity and how much trickery." The circumstances of Constantine's vision are related by Eusebius, not in his Ecclesiastical History but in his Life of Constantine (I, 28), which is now regarded as having been written after 337: "About the afternoon, when the day was already declining, (Constantine) said he actually saw with his own eyes in the sky the triumphal sign of the Cross, bodied forth in light, standing above the sun, and a writing attached to it which said 'By this conquer (τούτω νίκα): and amazement . . . seized him and all the soldiers who followed him . . . and became witnesses of the miracle."

the victor at Milan and celebrated his marriage with Constantia, Constantine's sister. This was in fact a repetition of Diocletian's policy of family alliances which was not, however, destined to last. The two Augusti took advantage of the meeting to discuss the general policy of the Empire and they agreed to oppose the hostile attitude of Maximin towards themselves. The first edict of toleration had been issued in 311 at Sardica (Sofia)[223] by that harsh persecutor of the Christians, Galerius, when he was ill and wished to propitiate the Christian God by friendly conduct towards His followers. Licinius who was Galerius's friend and later became Augustus, helped towards the promulgation of the decree, and in 313 he ratified both the contents of the Sardica decree and those of the decree (or rescript) called the decree of Nicomedia. Constantine was therefore not the first to think of toleration; but he offered no opposition to a decree which, while allowing freedom of worship to all religions alike, in fact restored their confiscated property to many Christian churches, represented a great step forward in this era of absolute government and permitted Christianity to spread with still greater vigour.

After their state business at Milan the two Augusti separated. In 313 Licinius sustained Maximin's attack in Thrace, between Adrianople and Heraclea, and defeated him. The formidable Maximin died while escaping from the field and thus relieved Licinius who, like some bloodthirsty Sultan of later times, took steps to kill the wife and the remaining children of Galerius. Evidently he was clearing the ground of every centre of suspicion because he feared the future.

The clash with Constantine was not long in coming, since the latter considered that Licinius had seized too much and that there should be a more just division. Constantine advanced into the Balkans and defeated Licinius twice, in Lower Pannonia and Thrace (314), but not decisively. He therefore postponed the final destruction of his opponent and accepted for the

---

223 The edict of Galerius has been translated from Lactantius (*De Morte Persecutorum*) by Eusebius (*Ecclesiastical History*, VIII, 17). The edict of Milan has not been separately preserved: it is, however, embodied in the decree of Nicomedia which Eusebius, once again, translated from Lactantius in his *Ecclesiastical History*, X, 5: "I, Constantine Augustus, and I, Licinius Augustus, . . . have, firstly, resolved to decree . . . that we grant both to Christians and to all others, freedom to choose and practice whatsoever religion they please."

time being an agreement by which Illyricum (the Balkan peninsula), except for Thrace up to the Danube, should be handed over to him. From that time onwards Illyricum ceased to include the eastern Balkans and included only the western half of the peninsula from Greece (including, be it noted, Crete) to Pannonia.

The Donatists

Before Constantine entered Illyricum and while he was still in Italy, there arose the famous Donatist question, which gave him some notion of Christian differences and obliged him for the first time to give his consideration to the solution of problems of this kind. Outwardly at least, Donatism began as a personal question, though it ended by becoming a social and racial one. The friends of Donatus were unwilling to accept the elected bishop of Carthage and sought the intervention of Constantine, who submitted the question first to a conference of bishops at Rome under the presidency of Bishop Miltiades, and subsequently, in 313, to a second Council at Arles in Gaul. When the decisions taken in both places turned out to be in favour of Donatus's adversary, they were at first disregarded; but later Constantine brought pressure to bear on the Donatists to make peace.

In 314 Silvester became bishop of Rome and Constantine, according to custom, sent him from time to time various gifts for a number of churches and especially for the shrine of the Apostles Peter and Paul.

In 316 Diocletian died, although not until he had been forced to realize that his policy of joint rulers and matrimonial alliances had failed and had not prevented war between the partners. Constantine bestowed divine honours upon him after the Roman custom; similarly he still did not discontinue his practice of striking coins with the inscription *Soli invicto*.

After Diocletian's death Constantine made his headquarters in Pannonia instead of at Trier in Gaul. It may be that the number of pagans there and the power of the wealthy Senators at Rome were not to his liking and caused him to remove to his native Illyricum. In 319 he moved further to Sardica, and remained there. From 321 he seems to have shown still greater favour to the Christians and their clergy and he

issued decrees in regard to their property. He evidently wished
to secure Christian support in his coming struggle against
Licinius.

The Engagements of 324

In 323, Under the pretext of striking at the Goths, Constantine invaded Thrace, which was one of the provinces of
Licinius. This incident and other causes brought on the desired encounter, in which the military forces arrayed against
each other were such as the ancient Roman world was never
to see again. In July 324 Constantine defeated Licinius near
Adrianople with an army of 130,000 men, Licinius on his side
having 165,000, including 15,000 cavalry. Licinius was forced to
fall back upon the powerful fortress of Byzantium while Constantine's son Crispus, whom his father had already proclaimed
Caesar, annihilated his rival's army at the Hellespont. This
blocked the transport of food supplies to Byzantium, which
Licinius had consequently to evacuate: he crossed over to
Chrysopolis on the opposite shore, where he was again defeated
by Constantine in September. At Nicomedia he was handed
over to Constantine who put him to death the following year,
and later his son as well—the child of a concubine, however,
and not of Constantine's own sister, Constantia.

Religious Unity

A powerful personality like that of Constantine was bound
to revolt against Diocletian's policy of joint rule and to seek
occasion to subdue his fellow-rulers. In contrast to Diocletian,
who had sought assistants, he had sufficient capacity to rule
the empire alone. But having restored its political unity, he
attempted to introduce religious unity as well. Like Aurelian
before him, Constantine believed in one supreme Diety, whom
up till this time he had identified with Apollo-Helios and whom
he gradually tended to identify with the Christian God. From
324 on he removed pagan symbols from his coinage and from
326 he placed on them the Labarum with the XP monogram.

Constantine's religious policy aimed at resolving Christian
differences, though without giving rise to conflict with the

pagans, to whom he showed himself equally tolerant. The Council of 324, which he summoned to solve the Arian problem, had for him a political and not a theological significance. Thus, in his religious policy also, Constantine did not follow Diocletian: he took account of realities and began the gradual approach to Christianity.

The Capital

One notable political act was the transference of the imperial capital to the East, after the example already given by Diocletian who had resided at Nicomedia. Constantine did not follow him exactly: he at first considered establishing his capital at Troy, which had mythological connections with Rome, but finally settled on Byzantium, the geographical and military importance of which he knew from first-hand experience, and also from the history of its three-year siege in the time of Septimius Severus (193-196 AD). Constantine fully appreciated, too, the commercial importance of Byzantium, lying between the Black Sea and the Aegean and between Europe and Asia. Apart from this, as an Illyrian he felt perhaps some dislike for Rome and wanted a capital nearer to his compatriots and to the Christians, whose power he recognized.

Constantine had already discerned the danger from Asia and wished to keep a better watch from Byzantium upon the movements of the Sarmatians and Goths on the Danube, as well as on those of the Persians whose strength had been shown in their capture of the Emperor Valerian in 260.

The choice of Constantinople as capital was also of particular significance for Greek history. The city not only developed economically and became the centre of world trade but promoted the development of the Greek world, to which it later gave the Byzantine Empire. The transference of the capital contributed to the gradual abandonment of the West to the Germanic peoples and the dissolution of the Western Roman Empire; on the other hand, it gradually delivered the East Roman Empire to the Greeks, who managed to retain it for over a thousand years. The moving of the capital has, therefore, a world-historical significance equal to that of Constantine's favorable policy towards Christianity.

On 11th May, 330, the inauguration of Constantinople took place, an occasion which continued to be celebrated in later years. The Emperor renamed Byzantium New Rome (it was later called the City of Constantine or "The City" pure and simple) and his intention was in fact to adorn and administer it after the pattern of Old Rome. He established a Senate, which embodied a few of the senators from the older city. A still larger number of new senators, however, was chosen from among known adherents to whom he gave financial support to enable them to maintain a suitable outward dignity. He likewise set up an Imperial Council (*Sacrum Consistorium*), in which higher officials, generals and other eastern notables took part. He enlarged the city's fortifications and granted it a certain degree of autonomy under its own prefect (Eparch), as well as relief from the provincial taxes which it was paying. For the adornment of the city he brought historical objects and works of art from various provinces and towns, some of which are still preserved, as for example the base of the famous Delphic tripod, offered by the Greeks after the battle of Plataea. Constantine also founded at Constantinople the Christian churches of the Holy Apostles, St. Irene, St. Sophia, and of the Power of God.

As a capital Constantinople grew rapidly and its growth helped to diminish the population of Old Rome, from which large numbers came to the New. The Greek element soon began to prevail and the city proved to be a powerful agent in the Helenization of the strangers who poured into it. As Lot has said,[224] had it not been for the removal of the capital Greek civilization would have been lost and we should have known it only from miserable remains.

Having solved the major problems of the unity of the Empire, Christianity and the capital, Constantine had few troubles to disturb him in his closing years. The endless quarrels between the adherents of Arius and those of Athanasius do not seem to have worried him, and he contented himself by taking decisions *ad hoc*, which as a result were

---

[224] F. Lot. *La fin du monde antique et le début Moyen Age*, 1927, p. 211: "Had it not been for this brilliant idea (of transferring the capital) Greek civilisation would have disappeared . . . it would have been known to us only from shapeless ruins."

often contradictory. On the Danube frontier the Sarmatians and Goths continued raiding but they were easily defeated in 334 and many thousands of Sarmatians were settled in the Empire, while the Goths undertook military duties on the frontiers in return for subsidies and food given them by the emperor. When the warlike Sapor II[225] of Persia (310-379) occupied Armenia in 334, Constantine proclaimed his nephew Hannibalianus king of that country, and it seems probably that the Persians were expelled by him. A little before 337 the emperor made peace with the Persians, whether because he had a presentiment of his own death or because he found it expedient to do so for some other reason.

On the 22nd May 337 Constantine died near Nicomedia, after receiving baptism from the Arian bishop of Nicomedia, Eusebius. He died relatively young, while his mother Helena lived to be over eighty. Possibly the quarrels and denunciations in his family had worn out his vitality. It is significant that he appointed his burial-place among the cenotaphs of the twelve Apostles.[226] In a sense he regarded himself as "equal with the Apostles (ἰσαπόστολος)." Such was this skilful statesman, who without being expressly philhellene, indeed perhaps without intending it, gave to the Greek world the power to transform the eastern Roman Empire into a Greek empire and to preserve the legacy of Greek civilization.

Religious Policy

Constantine, as we have said, recognized the increased power of Christianity as against extremely scattered pagan sects and wished to make use of it to the advantage of the Empire and of imperial unity. It was characteristic that at the Council of Arles in 313 he should have sought to induce the Christians not to oppose military service, as they had done up to that time, especially the Manicheans. Constantine certainly never

---

225 Constantine wrote to Sapor recommending a favourable attitude towards the Christians: "Favour them in accordance with your humane nature." (Eusebius. *Life of Constantine*, IV,13). On the persecution of the Christians under Sapor see H. Delehaye. "Les versions grecques des actes des martyrs persans sous Sapor II, in *Patr. Orient*, Vol. II (1907).

226 A. Phytrakis. *The Religion of Constantine the Great in the Last Years of his life*, 1945 (in Greek).

became a Christian, according to the old conception of Christian humility. He regarded and handled the problems of Christianity as a statesman, not as a theologian. The Christological question raised by Arius at Alexandria interested him, not in itself but because it gave rise to disturbances and irregularities in Egypt. After attempting to reconcile Arius and Athanasius through the mediation of Hosius, bishop of Cordoba, he was forced for the sake of peace to call the Council of Nicaea (325), and in his address he emphasized the evil effects of the bishops' quarrels.[227]

At the Council, in which many bishops took part who had suffered under the persecution of Diocletian, a duel took place between Arius and Athanasius, in which the former, on rationalist lines, and in order to secure the monotheistic principle, acknowledged Christ to have been created by God, while Athanasius, in order to preserve the dogmas of the Incarnation and the Redemption, acknowledged the Trinity of Father, Son and Holy Spirit. The Council adopted by a majority the view of the combative Greek deacon, Athanasius,[228] which was given its definitive shape more particularly at the Second Council in 381 and was then made binding upon the Church. The prevalence of Athanasius's views may be explained by the unshakable courage with which he defended them and

---

[227] Constantine came to the Council in person in order to secure the unity he desired and he addressed it in Latin, "while another interpreted." In private, however, he conducted gracious "conversations with each one, speaking Greek, since he was by no means ignorant of it". (Eusebius. *Life of Constantine*. III, 12). After the Council of Nicaea, Constantine wrote to the "Catholic Church of the Alexandrians", and spoke of his quest for peace: "The disagreements and cleavages, the tumults and the deadly poisons of discord, if I may call them so, have been overcome, at God's command, by the clear shining of truth. Therefore we all worship One by His name and believe Him to be. And that this might come about, by God's inspiration I assembled most of the bishops in the city of Nicaea . . ."

[228] On the discussions of the First Council see H. von Soden. "Die Entstehung des Christentums," in *Propyläen-Weltgeschichte* Vol. II (1931), p. 530. A small minority of bishops came from Europe (see Honigmann. *Byzantion*, Vol. XIV (1939), p. 17): *viz.* Protogenes of Sardica, Pistos of Marcianopolis, Cleonicus of Thebes, Pistos of Athens, and some others.

which brought him later to exile and to every form of humiliation.[229]

The Council of 325 was not followed by unbroken peace; nevertheless, the various differences took a harmless form. Constantine banished Arius and his fanatical follower Eusebius; but these men had sympathizers and friends at the imperial court, where the emperor's sister Constantia pleaded for the Arians. The exiles were therefore recalled and were restored to their offices by a decision of a Council held in 327. The irreconcilable Athanasius, who in 328 succeeded Alexander as bishop of Alexandria, refused to acknowledge Arius and these discords led to the condemnation of Athanasius at the Council of Tyre in 335 and to his banishment to Trier in Gaul. Clearly his stubborn persistence could not be tolerated by Constantine. His first banishment was, however, destined to help in imposing the doctrine of the 'Homoousios' [230] on the West. In the last years of Constantine's reign the Arians prevailed at court and it was to be an Arian bishop who baptized him.

The Council of 325 and the personal and other problems which arose out of it led Constantine into a still closer relationship with Christianity; it is not strange, therefore, that from 326 onwards he struck coins with the Labarum and the monogram and no longer bore the religious title *Invictus*, but the secular title *Victor*. He nevertheless still continued formally to bear the ancient Roman title of *Pontifex Maximus*, which Gratian later discarded, though without performing the actual functions attaching to it. The construction of the temple of Fortune (Tyche, the tutelary goddess of Rome) was finished before Constantine entered Constantinople, and he built no more pagan temples there. He forbade, for reasons of

229 The fighting spirit and the general attitude of Athanasius influenced Constantine who in turn influenced the Council. According to Lietzmann, "the Council decided as Constantine dictated." But the emperor perhaps regretted his policy later, since he imposed on Athanasius a sentence of exile.

230 As under Constantine the doctrine of the Holy Trinity was defined by the Council of 325, so under the Sassanid ruler of Persia, Sapor II, the full text of the Zoroastrian bible, the *Avesta*, was finally settled. Thenceforward the rivalry between Christianity and Zoroastrianism became acute. See Grousset, *L'Empire du Levant*, 1946, p. 67.

morality, the offering of sacrifices [231] at ancient shrines of ill reputation and he did not intervene to prevent the execution of the Neoplatonist Sopater. On the other hand, he helped the director (δαδοῦχος) of the Eleusinian mysteries to visit Egypt and its heathen temples, he showed favour to the pagan schools of Athens [232] and distributed corn to the pagan population of that city.

The statue of Constantine at Constantinople, which was probably erected by pagans and according to Hesychius "shone like the sun" (under the guise, therefore, of Apollo-Helios) on its porphyry pillar (which still survives today in a semi-ruinous condition was retained by him but he placed on it the sign of the cross and thus made it to some extent Christian.[233] He forbade the placing of his statues in pagan shrines ("he forbade by law the setting up of his image in the temples of idols").

Although he had been baptized as a genuine Christian before he died, shortly after his death he was proclaimed *Divus* by the senate, and he was later, in addition canonized as a saint by the Christians. He was, however, far from seeking the full Roman apotheosis; on the contrary, he chiefly employed Christian epithets and symbols. He struck coins with the aureoled head, his palace was termed "sacred"(*sacrum palatium*) as also was the Imperial Council (*sacrum consistorium*), and one of his Finance Ministers was called "Count of the Sacred Largesse" (*comes sacrarum largitionum*), the other being called "Count of the Privy Purse" (*comes rerum privatarum*).

These apparent contradictions for which Constantine has been severely condemned by many historians, are explicable only if they are considered from the political angle as the actions of a statesman who was gradually moving towards Christianity, while still paying a good deal of regard to the

---

[231] According to Eusebius (*Life of Constantine*, IV, 25) "By a sequence of laws and ordinances he forbade generally all sacrifices to idols, all working of oracles, all erection of wooden statues and the celebration of secret mysteries."

[232] Graindor, in the periodical *Byzantion*, Vol. III (1927), p. 209.

[233] Th. Preger. "Konstantinos-Helios," in *Hermes*, Vol. XXXVI (1901), p. 457; V. Stephanides. "Constantine the Great and Emperor-worship," in *Annual of the Society for Byzantine Studies*, Vol. VIII (1931) (in Greek), p. 214 ff.

pagans as well.[234]

Christianity had begun to make greater headway ever since its persecutor, the Emperor Valerian, had been taken prisoner by the Persians (260) and his successor Gallienus had been forced in consequence to show indulgence to the Christians. Paganism, on the other hand, had gradually sunk into a decline, to which its poverty had contributed. The last inscription recording an Olympic victory is of the year 261, after which date the moneys needed to pay for this commemoration either ran out or were not forthcoming. Various generals, emperors and private citizens plundered the ancient temples, and Constantine himself by seizing the gold from pagan temples found most of what he needed to coin a sound gold currency (the *solidus aureus*) and to restore the monetary system by degrees to its old flourishing condition in place of the system of barter to which the economy of the ancient world had fallen in the third century AD.

The gold standard now finally imposed by Constantine after the earlier attempts of Aurelian and Diocletian was maintained by Byzantium until the eleventh century and proved to be one of the principal factors contributing to its power.

Constantine's achievement lies, precisely, in his having recognized the practical fact that not even Diocletian's persecutions could arrest the advance of Christianity, and by his rapprochement with it he neutralized its opposition. It may have been that his utilization of the funds of the ancient temples helped to lead him more rapidly in the direction of Christianity, which to him meant, essentially, monotheism and which supplied him with the *summus deus* he spoke of so often.

If we explained Constantine's development in this way, we need not necessarily disbelieve in his Christian convictions but we need not credit him with theological knowledge. His Christianity appears not only from what has already been said but also from the following facts. The early decrees of Sardica and Nicomedia regarding religious toleration enforced the award to Christian priests of numerous privileges which pagan priests already enjoyed, tax exemption, for example, freedom from

[234] According to E. Schwartz. *Kaiser Konstantin und die christliche Kirche,* 1936, p 88, Constantine himself came in time to acknowledge Christianity.

requisitions and from compulsory service. But Constantine personally made large donations to the Church, Eusebius tells us (*Life of Constantine*, VI, 28): "To the Churches of God he gave in abundance all manner of choice things, bestowing lands on one and on another gifts of corn for the service of the poor, of orphan children and destitute widows . . . and especially singled out for the greatest honours those who devoted their lives to the divine philosophy (*i.e.* the monks)."

In addition to economic privileges he also bestowed legal privileges on the clergy, in so far as he allowed appeal to be made from the law courts to the bishops. Apart from this the bishops had jurisdiction over the clergy, and the recognition of the right of asylum gave the bishop legal ground for intervention. Generally, it can be said that the development of canon law and the definition of the episcopal power start from the Council of Nicaea.[235]

The right to receive donations and legacies proved very profitable for the Church. They enabled it to build up its property and to undertake its great humanitarian work of caring for orphans, widows, the aged, the sick, prisoners and the burial of foreign dead. The solidarity and mutual aid established among Christians by the *agape* of the early centuries were systematically organized from the fourth century on and this was partly made possible by the right given to the Church to inherit and receive gifts. Constantine himself followed this humanitarian example and not only distributed food to the people (corn, bread and oil) in the manner of ancient Rome but also distributed money to the poor. His mother Helena followed suit at Constantinople and in her journey to Jerusalem to discover the precious wood of the Cross.[236]

Legislation

In other respects too Constantine's legislature and political work came under the influence of Christianity and these must

[235] H. von Soden. *Die Entstehung des Christentums*, p. 539.

[236] Eusebius (*Life of Constantine*, III, 44 '(on Helena) and *ibid.* I. 43): "He made all manner of distributions of money to those who were in need . . . and he cared, in place of a father, for those who had the misfortune to be orphans. In relieving the solitude of widow women he made domestic provision for them and he even went so far as to join in marriage to wealthy men of his acquaintance girls who had been orphaned by the loss of their parents."

be noted here. Thus, for example, he forbade the execution of the death penalty by crucifixion and relaxed some of the various harsher penalties. He reduced the power of the *pater--familias* (who had earlier had the power of life and death (*vitae necisque*) over his children) over children and women. Any child (the legitimate, but not the illegitimate) was entitled, even during his father's lifetime, to inherit a third of his mother's estate. If the father's property was confiscated, the mother's was kept for the family. If the mother died, the children inherited all but a third of her estate, which went to the father. The decrees inflicting penalties on celibates were cancelled and concubinage was forbidden to married men.[237]

In this way, under the influence of Christianity, and perhaps of prevailing Eastern practice which he took into account in his legislation, Constantine helped to raise the status of the family, which ever since the time of Augustus, that is to say from the time when concubinage had been allowed in order to encourage the procreation of children, had suffered a great depreciation.

Constantine's improvement of the law was one of his first achievements. In effect, the period of the creation of Greco-Roman law under Christian influences begins from this date. The Theodosian Codex starts from 312. About three hundred fragments of Constantine's laws and decrees have survived.[238] Unfortunately this powerful personality never directed his attention to the social situation which found its sole relief in the humanitarian social service of the Christian Church. The detailed decrees of Constantine regarding the collection of taxes in kind, and his introduction of the *chrysargyron* [239] show

---

[237] See J. Maurice. *Constantin le Grand. L'Origine de la civilisation chrétienne,* 1924, p. 126. Crispus, the illegitimate son of Constantine, was condemned by the Roman Senate in 326 for breaking the law regarding concubinage, on the denunciation of his step mother, Fausta (Maurice, *op. cit.,* p. 185). When Helena, who was fond of Crispus and disliked Fausta, denounced her for slandering him out of desire to destroy him in favour of her own children, Fausta too was executed upon an accusation of adultery. (See also H. Lietzmann. *Geschichte der alter Kirche,* Vol. III (1938), p. 127).

[238] Palanque. *Constantin,* p. 381.

[239] The tax known as the *chrysargyron,* collected every five years, was undoubtedly introduced with a view to strengthening the gold standard and the gold currency.

the crushing weight of taxation and render credible all that
Zosimus says against it.[240] This same policy led him to take no
steps even on behalf of the wretched agriculturists; indeed
in 331 he even revived a law of Diocletian's in order to force
labourers to undertake compulsory work.[241] The social situation was rendered still worse by Constantine's lavish expenditure on public services, the building of churches, martyrs'
shrines and so forth.[242]

Two other decrees of Constantine's time may be mentioned.
The Day of the Sun (*solis dies*) was reentitled the Lord's Day
(Κυριακή) and was officially fixed as the Christian day *par
excellence*. Again, perhaps towards the end of Constantine's
reign, the day marked by legend as that of the birth of Mithras,
December 25th, was appointed in the West as the date (hither-
to unknown) of the birth of Christ. These examples show how
—in accordance with the spirit of Constantine himself, the
worship and the traditions of Helios-Mithras were fused with
Christianity. The *summus deus* of Constantine was first Apollo-
Helios and then Christ. Julian was to reintroduce Apollo-
Helios.

Despite his personal failings and the irascibility of his nature,
which all too easily brought even those of his own family to
their deaths, Constantine the Great was one of the greatest
generals and statesmen in the history of the world. He was
never defeated, and he always overcame forces much superior
to his own. Gradually and almost without bloodshed he led
the world from the old religions and from its various heretical
sects to Christian orthodoxy. He guided the Roman Empire
out of the *cul-de-sac* of the third century, strengthened it by
transferring its capital to Constantinople and gave it into the
hands of the Greeks who defended it for a thousand years,
and with it Europe, against the barbarians of Asia.[243]

[240] Zosimus, II, 38: "He (Constantine) introduced the *chrysargyron* tax
on all those who were conducting trade throughout the country. Mothers
sold their children and fathers hired their daughters out to prostitution,
being driven to gather for the collectors of the *chrysargyron* the money
derived from these earnings of theirs."

[241] Piganiol. *op. cit.*, p. 298.

[242] A curious instance is the renovation of the city of Cirta in Africa,
which was thenceforward renamed Constantine.

Constantius II

Constantine had, while still alive, proclaimed his sons Constantine II, Constans and Constantius Caesars, and had ceded to the first the government of Gaul, Spain and Britain, to the second Italy and Africa and to the third Asia and Egypt. Illyricum he had given to his nephew Dalmatius. After his death, however, a military revolution broke out against Dalmatius in the course of which, besides Dalmatius himself, the brothers of Constantine the Great, Dalmatius and Julius Constantius and five other nephews, including that Hannibalianus whom Constantine had made King of Armenia, were all killed. When this fearful massacre took place Constantius was at Constantinople: it is therefore permissible to suspect that he himself or his faction had devised it.

The Roman Empire could not expect to be greatly strengthened by such an inhuman ruler, who recalls the earlier age of the Praetorians or the later age of the Sultans. The greater the material power, when it is unaccompanied by moral scruple, the greater the injury it inflicts on a nation. Constantius soon came into conflict with his brother Constantine II, whom he destroyed. In 350 Constans [244] was murdered in the rising of the German senior officer Magnentius, and Constantius was thus left as sole Emperor. He soon, however, saw the need for some kind of family support and summoned from Cappadocia, where he had kept him in sequestration with Julian, his cousin Gallus, whom he proclaimed Caesar and despatched to the West. But this partnership did not last long: Gallus too was murdered in 354, on account of the tyrannical nature of his government. The reason given seems plausible, but was this

---

[243] M. Volonakis has written a long work of 703 pages on Constantine and his successors down to Jovian under the title *A History of the Middle Ages.* Vol. I *From the Accession of Constantine the Great to Jovian* (306-364 AD). 1947. The book is illustrated with a number of pictures, maps and tables.

[244] At this point an interesting inscription may be recorded from the reign of Constantius and Constans, after the murder of Constantine II: "In commemoration of the safety and victory of our sovereigns Constantine and Constans, the invincible Emperors, this bridge was rebuilt from its foundations, in the governorship of Flavius Hierocles, who is in all things devoted to Their Divinities (sic)." (*Supplementum Epigraphicum Graecum,* Vol. VII, 1934, No. 256).

in fact the real reason for the murder or the abnormal, indeed pathological, temper of Constantius?

The revolt of Magnentius caused Constantius considerable trouble. It is even said that he called the Germans into Gaul in order to embarrass the rebel leader. Finally, in 351, a major engagement [245] was fought in Pannonia on the Drave, a tributary of the Danube, in which the forces of Constantius which were about double those of his opponent (80,000 men with large numbers of heavy-armed cavalry) crushed Magnentius, although both sides sustained and caused terrible casualties.

In this history of Constantius it is hard to explain from the psychological point of view his devotion to his wife Eusebia, the first Greek empress of Byzantium. Who knows what sacrifices and what painful efforts it cost this intelligent woman to hold his love? To her pleading was due the recall of Julian from his internment in Cappadocia and his despatch to Athens, and later his proclamation as Caesar and his mission to the West. While still in his youth, Julian distinguished himself as a general; he defeated the Alamanni near Strasbourg in 357 and the Franks elsewhere, and showed himself, in addition, a wise and humane administrator. But these successes and the intrigues of spies aroused the mistrust of Constantius who wished to transfer him to the East. An opportunity was afforded by the Persian war and the capture and destruction of Amida by the Persians. Constantius asked Julian for troops but Julian refused to send them, since he needed them against the Germans and had no desire to meet the fate of Gallus. In 361, while Constantius was on his way back from his eastern campaign and planning to march against Julian, the latter set off from the West for Constantinople. Any encounter between them was, however, forestalled, since Constantius died in Cilicia on the way, and Julian came to Constantinople in his stead.

Religious Questions

The bloody reign of Constantius was not to have a salutary effect on the Empire. The religious problem of Arianism inevitably claimed the attention of the Emperor, who

[245] Stein. *op.cit.*, p. 217.

had not the least idea how to deal with it. He began by allowing Athanasius, whom Constantine had exiled, to return to his post from Gaul. But the intransigence and pugnacity of Athanasius gave rise to fresh disturbances and to his deposition by a local council at Antioch: he was thus compelled to flee to Rome. The Pope was ranged on his side, while the death of Eusebius of Nicomedia raised the question of a new bishop for Constantinople. This accumulation of problems caused Constantius to call a new Council at Sardica (Sofia) in 343 to re-examine the situation. Finally, he was obliged to allow the return of Athanasius to Alexandria. But by degrees the Arians succeeded in engaging his sympathies and in arousing his anger against Athanasius whose arrest he ordered. When Athanasius resisted, an army of five thousand men was required to surround him in a certain church, from which even so he contrived to escape to safety with the help of fanatical followers. Thenceforward Constantius leaned towards Arianism.

The Donatist question also revived under Constantius, while Constans was still alive. When Constans was vainly attempting to come to terms with the Orthodox faction, he launched a severe persecution against the Donatists in Africa; he closed their churches, banished their followers and finally forbade their cult. Donatus himself is said to have died in exile at that time. These persecutions in no way reduced the hersey, which later played a part in political issues also, precisely because it concealed social and racial problems beneath a religious covering.

It is easy to understand that a cruel character like that of Constantius, irritated incessantly by religious problems, readily resorted to Caesaropapism. For the same reason he showed equal readiness to resort to force against Athanasius and the Donatists and annulled the decision of the local Council held in Italy regarding the exemption of Church properties from taxation.

CHAPTER IX

JULIAN, VALENS AND THEODOSIUS

Flavius Claudius Julianus

Julian [246] was born in 331 AD, the son of Julius Constantius (himself the son of Theodora, the lawful wife of Constantius I) and his second wife, Basilina, in whose honour he later founded the city of Basilinopolis near Nicaea. Julian lost his mother at an early age and was left an orphan; and on the death of Constantine the Great (337), Julian's father, Constantius, was murdered, together with numerous brothers and nephews, with the connivance or even at the instigation of the Emperor Constantius. Julian was, in consequence, left without any of his family about him, the only survivors being himself and his brother Gallus. The sole piece of good fortune in Julian's boyhood was that a good tutor was found for him, the Scythian eunuch Mardonius, who undertook his education with affection and was the first to teach him Homer and other ancient masters.

The suspicious nature of Constantius caused him to dispatch his two small cousins, Gallus and Julian, to an imperial estate in Cappadocia, so that they might pursue their studies far from the world and from the stir of politics; and Constantius himself paid a visit to confirm that his two kinsmen were shut away. This relegation began to breed in Julian's mind an antipathy to Constantius and to Christianity. Fortunately for him Cappadocia afforded an excellent library of Greek and Christian authors, with whom Julian passed the period of his isolation; he had moreover the leisure to make his own choice and to establish his preference for the writers of antiquity, and with them, for paganism.

He later had opportunities to get to know various pagans of note, such as Libanius at Nicomedea and, at Pergamon,

[246] J. Bidez. *La Vie de l'Empereur Julien*, Paris 1930.

Aidesius, the disciple of the Neoplatonist Iamblichus, with other mystical divines, whom he made his friends and from whom he acquired a closer knowledge of the contemporary notions of the Neoplatonic philosophy and its special mystic rites or mysteries. He likewise visited Ilion in the Troad and worshipped at the tomb of Achilles (a typical gesture towards paganism); and there he found the doctrinally somewhat dubious Bishop Pegasus, who expounded to him the sacred monuments of the ancient city.

In 354 Julian's brother Gallus was murdered at the bidding of Constantius and Julian was left as the sole member of his family, becoming thereafter more and more closely attached to his new pagan friends. Of all Constantine's family only Eusebia, the wife of Constantius, a Greek from Salonica, felt for Julian and helped him. That he was grateful to her appears from the tribute which he wrote.[247] On the initiative of Eusebia, whom Constantius loved and honoured greatly, he was sent to Athens, where he stayed a few months and got to know not only the Neoplatonic philosophers, Proairesius, Himerius and the rest, but also such Christian students as Basil, later called the Great, and Gregory of Nazianzus. It should be noted that Julian's visits to the ancient cities of Hellas greatly moved him owing to the abandonment of many of the temples and the neglect, and even persecution, of their religion. With his generous mind, Julian already felt an inner need to help in the restoration of the temples of Greece, a country for which he continually showed his affection.[248] Although Athens still retained many memorials of antiquity, yet even among these a vivid impression was made on Julian

---

[247] J. Bidez. *L'Empereur Julien, Oeuvres Completes,* Vol. I, p. 73. ff., pp. 82,87, of the same volume. It is said of Eusebia, "Her family were completely Greek, of the purest Greek descent, and her native city was the chief town of Macedonia. In modesty she was above Evadne, the wife of Capareus and the Thessalian Laodamia."

[248] Bidez. I, pp. 92, 12: " . . . for we who live in the regions of Thrace and Ionia are children of Greece, and any of us who is not utterly insensitive longs to hail our forefathers and to embrace the land itself." And p. 39, 14: ". . . and now what fullness of speach is it in my mind to utter, if not the praise of my beloved Greece, which it is impossible to mention without admiring it all?"

by the destruction and spoliation inflicted by Sulla and other Romans, and later (267) by the Goths.

In 355 Constantius proclaimed Julian Caesar, since he had no longer any hope of children by his beloved Eusebia. At the same time the emperor gave his sister Helen in marriage to Julian, who was then sent to govern Gaul. This marriage and the dignity of Caesar showed that Constantius had thenceforward accepted Julian as co-ruler and as his fellow-ruler and probable successor. But the marriage was not a happy one, since Julian was not in love with Helen, who in fact died very shortly after, not long after Eusebia.

This appointment as Caesar gave Julian the opportunity of developing all his abilities as a military and political leader. The Alamanni and the Franks, Germanic peoples, had made great inroads into Gaul and had contributed to the wretched state of the country, which was due on the one hand to the deep poverty existing among the masses, and on the other to the building up of large landed estates, whose owners bought up the holdings of the poor for a dish of lentils. Over a space of three years Julian waged hard but successful campaigns both against the Alamanni (356) and against the Franks (358-9). Three times he crossed the Rhine and forced the Alamanni and other Germans to return twenty thousand prisoners, for whose welfare he took particular care,[249] as he also did for that of the devastated areas.[250] He also made the Germans responsible for rebuilding the towns. Had it not been for Julian, as Bidez rightly allows,[251] the Franks would have occupied Gaul at that time, that is to say a century earlier than they did: they finally occupied it in the fifth century.

Julian also employed himself in improving conditions in Gaul and tried to relieve the poor from the financial charges which the rich had succeeded in imposing upon them. It is clear, in fact, that he had already come to know and to practice Mithraism, which made it a duty to strive for virtue and justice. He had always been a very ready fighter, just as he had always been a strongly ascetic type of man.

While in Gaul, he never ceased to maintain his relations and

249 Zosimus III, 4, 4-5, 1, *Julien* (ed. Bidez) I, 1, p. 227.

250 E. Stein. *Geschichte des spätrömischen Reiches*, Vol. I, (1928), p. 223.

251 Bidez. *La Vie de l'Empereur Julien*, p. 162.

his correspondence with the Neoplatonists: he seems, further, to have summoned some of them to Paris,[252] where he resided in preference to the city of Trier (Augusta Treverorum) where the Caesars and Augusti of the Roman Empire had previously lived. The Empress Eusebia sent him "books of the philosophers and good writers, with those of many orators and poets," and thus made of "the land of the Celts" (Gaul) "a museum of the Greek books."[253]

Julian's successes, in whatever version they may have been represented to the suspicious Constantius by the swarm of spies and agents who followed him by higher command, aroused the Emperor's opposition. First, Julian's valued counsellor and best administrator, Sallust, was ordered to leave Gaul and proceed to Constantinople; and Julian wrote "A Consolation to the most excellent Sallust on his departure." After the death of Eusebia (359) Julian's position became difficult, and he began to consider how he could proceed against Constantius. More particularly, after the death of his wife Helen, his ties of kinship with Constantius weakened.

The Greco-Persian war of 359 hastened the breach between the two rival cousins. The Persian commander took Amida (Diarbekir), sacrificing to its gallant defenders thirty thousand Persians, but taking prisoner six legions of the brave fighters who had held Amida for two months. This great loss to the Roman Empire naturally roused Constantius to thoughts of retribution and he began to make preparations to this end and to mobilize an army. At a time when the incursion of the Picts and Scots into Roman Britain had made it necessary for Julian to cross over there, Constantius demanded troops from him for his new war against the Persians. Julian resolved to disobey and his resistance thus began. Despite the impetuousness of his character Constantius showed caution and sought in vain for some compromise solution. Julian, however, having taken the advice of the physician Orivasius and other pagan friends, and having performed various mystic rites through his pagan priests, decided to take up the struggle against Con-

252 Zosimus, IX, 1. "Of Julian's stay in Paris (this is a small town in Germany)."

253 *Julien.* (ed.Bidez) I, 1, p. 98

stantius, whom at other times in moments of gratitude he had praised.

From Gaul he came to Sirmium in Pannonia (the modern Sremska Mitrovica in Yugoslavia), the capital and keypoint of Illyricum, thence to Naissus (Nish), the cradle of the family of Constantine the Great. Everywhere he was preceded by the fame of his military ability, which made it impossible for the imperial armies to stand against him. The rapid improvement in the administration of the countries which he occupied, by the lightening of economic burdens and by better government, roused enthusiasm for him. At Nish Julian learned of the death of Constantius (361), who had been baptized at the last moment, after his father's example. He there received the submission of the army of Asia and was assured that his enemies were powerless to prevent his accession to the throne. For this he gave thanks to the pagan gods with sacrifices and showered honours upon the priests and other pagans whom he had about him as counsellors.

In Constantinople Julian gave Constantius burial as Emperor and escorted his body as far as the Church of the Holy Apostles where it was interred; but he also allowed the Senate to hail the Christian Constantius as "divine" (divus) after the custom of the ancient Roman apotheosis. He clearly considered it of value to continue this antique practice.

After his installation as Emperor, Julian characteristically convoked a court of justice at Chalcedon, which within a few weeks tried those who had been guilty of the death of his brother Gallus and of various other offenses committed by the court of Constantius, No one, however, was condemned on grounds of religion.

As an admirer of the Stoic Marcus Aurelius, whose *Meditations* he frequently read, Julian brought a certain degree of simplicity into the court. He simplified the formalities which had been introduced into the Byzantine court from the period of Diocletian and on the Sassanid model, and he put on end to the enormous host of spies and other superfluous functionaries. He gave the Court more of a Greek character, more particularly by summoning to it not only Themistius, the Neoplatonic counsellor of Constantius, but other men of learning as well, his own friend the pagan physician Orivasius, the physician Caesarius, the brother of Gregory Nazianzene, and others.

Religious Policy

Julian inaugurated his new religious policy at a very early stage, a policy shaped by the Neoplatonic philosophy, by his acquaintance with the philosophers Libanius, Themistius, and others, and also by Mithraism, with which he had perhaps formed a closer acquaintance in the camps of the West. It was not a question of reintroducing the ancient religion of any given period but rather the religion of a single god under the form of Helios-Mithras, to whom he built a temple and performed the sacrifices of a bull and ram (*Taurobolia* and *Kriobolia*), the purificatory sacrifices of the Persian god.[254] The warlike followers of Mithras were useful to him in many ways in his struggle on behalf of the new paganism.

Among Julian's first ordinances were the ordinances on religious toleration which without persecution permitted a strengthening of the position of paganism. He appointed pagans to state offices and protected the temples and the temple property which had been appropriated by the Christians, and thus brought back to tolerable living the wretched priests and other servitors of the ancient religion.

Julian's new policy did not indeed provoke much in the way of revolt, since at the outset he proceeded with caution, but it did provoke opposition; and it may be readily understood that the greater this opposition was, the more incensed and fanatical the pugnacious Julian became.

In June 362 he issued a law which prescribed that teachers must be men of good conduct, which, to Julian's mind, Christians who had abandoned the faith of their fathers could never

254 In his attack on Christianity he writes *inter alia*: "Are you alone insensitive to the beam which strikes downward from the Sun? Are you alone ignorant that summer and winter come from him and that you receive life and movement from him? And she who is by him and from him and is the creator of all things, the Moon, do you not realize how many blessings she confers on the city? And do you dare to worship neither of these gods, but instead believe that Jesus, whom neither you nor your fathers have ever seen, must needs be the Divine Word?" (*Julien* (ed. Bidez) I, 2, p. 190).

be.[255] It followed that only pagan teachers ought to teach the
ancient authors and it must be confessed that this measure had
at least a certain logic about it. How could the Christians teach
the ancient writers well? It is to be noted that Julian also
had a definite programme for the schools; he wished for "in-
struction not merely in words but in morals," (Julian I, 2. p.
73), he wished teachers to believe what they taught and he
wished the moral philosophers Plato, Aristotle, Zeno and
Chrysippus to be taught, but not poets like Hipponax or Archi-
lochus or the Epicurean philosophers.

Before employing the power of the state against the Christians, Julian made war upon them in his writings and by rid-
icule at their expense. Thus for example, in addition to his
attacks upon Christ (see note 254) he strongly condemned the
monastic life (Vol. I, 2, p. 155): "There are some who, although
man is by nature a political and domestic animal, prefer the
wilderness to the town, being given over to evil demons, by
whom they are led into this hatred of the human race. Many
of these men have already gone so far as to devise chains and
collars: thus on every hand they are driven on by the evil
spirit to whom they have deliberately surrendered themselves..."[256]

Julian's mind, inflamed by ancient Greek culture, could
hardly fail to look with contempt on Christianity and to consider it a barbarous thing. He himself boasted, "I am a Greek,"
and in saying this of course he referred not only to his devotion
to the religion of ancient Greece but to his general education
and outlook, which he considered superior to those of Christianity.

But although he fought against Christianity, he imitated
those points in it which he considered useful. Thus, for example, he tried to organize a pagan clergy on the Christian
model, and he appointed priests and chief priests. The pagan
priests were to offer prayer three times a day and to learn by

255 This question later gave rise to many discussions and rhetorical dis-
quisitions: "What reply should a Christian man of letters give on being
forbdiden by Julian the Apostate to read Greek books?"

256 About the singing of psalms and making the sign of the cross, he
writes (I. 2. p. 86): "The height of religious wisdom with them (the
Christians) consists in two things — whistling to the demons and sketch-
ing the cross on their foreheads."

heart the hymns appropriate to each of the gods.[257] He recognized that Christianity derived advantage from its philanthropic work ("this godless creed [he meant Christianity] swells its numbers by its charity to strangers and its care for the burial of the dead") and he recommended the foundation of charitable establishments, in which not only pagan but Christians also might find relief. To the pagan chief priest of Galatia he wrote, "Set up numerous hostelries in every city so that strangers may enjoy our bounty, and not only those of our own persuasion but any who lack money." "Above all," he wrote (I. 2. p. 156), "we must practice benevolence, since many other blessings follow on it, the choicest and greatest being the favour of the gods."

War with Persia

Julian could not remain indifferent to the hostilities which Sapor (310-379), the warlike leader of the Persians, had begun and in the course of which he had captured the strong fortress of Amida. He therefore decided to undertake the necessary punitive campaign against him, but his execution of it was peculiar. Several times in the course of his march he visited remote temples and conducted propaganda on behalf of paganism; he encountered resistance, however, and was forced to resort to violent measures, abandoning his policy of religious toleration and becoming fanatical. From Nicaea in Bithynia he pressed on to Ancyra (Ankara), from which place he paid his respects to the temple of Cybele at Pessinus, regarding which he wrote (I. 2. p. 146): "I am ready to help Pessinus, if the people will make the Mother of the Gods look with favour on them; but if they neglect her . . . not to speak too harshly, let them beware lest they taste our displeasure too."

From Asia Minor he descended to Antioch where he was much moved at meeting Libanius, who was among the deputation sent by the city to welcome him. At the intercession of Libanius he distributed corn to the poor of the city and granted other forms of economic relief, although the Christians angered him by their attitude of hostility which provoked

---

[257] See Bidez. *La Vie de l'Empereur Julien*, p. 270 & ff.

him to write his *Misopogon* (the Beard-hater) against them.
When, after Julian's visit to the temple of Apollo-Helios in a
suburb of Antioch, the Christians hastened to burn it, being
further set on to it by his fanatical followers, he decided to
make reprisals and to use force against the Christians. As
his feeling against the Christians grew stronger, he failed to
enter the city of Nisibis and gave it the protection it sought,
simply because the inhabitants were Christians; and in Edessa
he behaved badly to the Christians.

He sought pretexts for the destruction of Christian churches
and praised the zeal of the pagans of Emesa in destroying
Christian tombs.[258] He punished the outbreaks of Christians
against pagans, while treating their counterparts with indif-
ference. His antipathy to the Christians led him into sympathy
with the Jews, in contrast with the antisemitic policy of the
earlier Roman Emperors. He sympathized with the conservatism of the Jews and with their devotion to the ways of their
forefathers, and he rebuilt the Temple of Solomon. All this
political action did not, however, prevent his making thorough
preparations for the war and making ready a thousand vessels
for the transport of troops and supplies down the river Tigris—
vessels which he was to be obliged to burn as they were unable
to navigate the strong currents.[259] Julian's old and well-tried
friend, Sallust, seeing the difficulties attending the river passage, which were fully exploited by the Persians, advised a
timely retreat, which Julian hesitated to undertake. It was a
fatal moment. When the order was given to form a line of
battle there was a panic in one division of the army; Julian
hastened towards it but was wounded, it is uncertain how
(363). There was a certain pathos in the last moments of the
emperor who was now compelled to abandon so many visionary
schemes. But perhaps his death was not inopportune, since
the bigoted policy on which he had embarked ever since
Antioch was bound to cause him grave trouble. Julian was

[258] See Bidez. *ibid.*, p. 296 ff.

[259] According to Joannes Lydus (*On the Months* IV, 118), Julian was
duped by two Persian spies, who "having mutilated their ears and nostrils".
told him that, in order to obtain a swift revenge on the King of the
Persians who had been the cause of their mutilation, they were eager to
help the Emperor. Julian believed these spies, who guided him "into a
dry and waterless defile" and so to disaster.

no political realist like his uncle Constantine; an enthusiast
and a dreamer, he imagined that he could turn back the river
of history to its source. The most he might have succeeded in
doing, if he had lived, would perhaps have been to delay the
spread of Christianity to those provinces which were still
pagan. Julian's failure was further aided by the fanatical
priests who followed in his train and made him a religious
zealot.

Flavius Claudius Joviannus (Jovian)

It is significant that both Julian's friends and his enemies
concurred in choosing as his successor a moderate Christian,
Jovian, an Illyrian from Pannonia. Jovian made haste to patch
up a peace and succeeded in doing so by ceding to the Persians
the provinces beyond the Tigris, Nisibis and fifteen other for-
tresses in Mesopotamia. Ephriam the Syrian left Nisibis, his
native city, at that time and set up an Aramaic school in Edessa.

On its homeward march the army brought the body of
Julian to Tarsus in Cilicia, where they buried it. The following epigram was placed on the tomb:

> Julian from the headlong Tigris lies here, both
> a good Emperor and a mighty man-at-arms.[260]

Pagan historians like Zosimus, Eunapius and Ammianus
Marcellinus, who wrote a detailed account of Julian, extol his
virtues and his achievements, while the Christians, Ephraim
the Syrian, Gregory Nazianzene and others, have held up
his name to the execration of posterity. It is only in modern
times that a cooler judgment has been passed on him.

After Julian's death proceedings were taken against his
more fanatical followers, more particularly the priest Maximus of Ephesus, who was killed. Libanius himself, who was
in other respects so highly regarded by all, was harassed by
the Christians, who now became aggressive towards the pagans.

Before Jovian reached Constantinople he had already begun
cancelling Julian's ordinances in favour of paganism and against

260 Zosimus, IV. 3. 4.

Christianity; but in 364 while he was still in Bithynia and was making for the capital, he suddenly died.

Flavius Valens

The generals and highest officers of state consulted together at Nicaea regarding the election of an emperor and agreed on the person of Valentinian, and Illyrian from Pannonia and an officer of the Imperial Guard (*palatinae scholae*), who shortly afterwards chose as co-ruler for the East his brother Valens. Valentinian was occupied in the West with the war against the Alamanni and with the war against the Sarmatians on the Danube. In 375 he died and was succeeded by his young son, Gratian, who had received his education from the poet and professor of rhetoric Ausonius at Bordeaux (Bordigala).

Valens had assisted his brother in preparing the frontier fortifications (*Limes*) from the Danube to the Rhine. With Valentinian, and with Gratian after him, he took certain steps on behalf of the farming population, as well as enacting other measures of relief — perhaps on the instigation of Ausonius, and at Constantinople he built an aqueduct which still survives. He likewise attempted to establish *defensores civitatis*— protectors of the poor against the powerful — and fought against the so-called "protection" of the poor by the wealthy. Any countryman who sought "protection" was punished by being beaten with rods and the 'protector" (*patronus*) was heavily fined.[261]

Although Gratian and the uneducated Valens may have begun by being impartial in the matter of religion, they were gradually roused by the provocative zeal of Ambrose, who was vehemently attacking Arianism, to take sides with him. After the death of Athanasius in 373 the most eminent theologian in the East and the enemy of Arianism was Basil the Great, whom Valens threatened without succeeding in forcing him by threats to retreat.

Arianism scored great successes among the Goths who had descended on the Danube from the Baltic. They had received

261 E. Stein. *Geschichte des spätrömischen Reiches*, Vol. I. (1928), p. 277 ff.

it from Ulfilas, who was of Cappadocian extraction on his father's side [262] and had been ordained by Eusebius of Nicomedia. Ulfilas translated the Bible into the Gothic dialect— his translation being the oldest extant monument of the German language.

The Goths

In 364 the Goths, who were now under pressure from other peoples owing to the westward movement of the Huns,[263] began crossing the Danube in quest of settlement and the right to live within the Roman Empire. Valens transferred his residence to Marcianopolis (where Themistius gave an address before him in 368) and agreed to their settling since he had great hopes of enlisting them and thus securing a reinforcement for his army.

It proved quite impossible, however, to effect the settlement of the Goths south of the Danube without a hitch. The officials charged with the allocation of land and food supplies often appropriated them, while the Goths, for their part, were looking for an excuse to plunder. In circumstances such as these, it took little to set them in revolt and the Imperial troops were unable to hold even the passes of the Balkan range. Valens, who was then in the East, was obliged to come to

[262] See Philostorgius. *Ecclesiastical History*, Bidez's edition, II. 15: "Among these prisoners there were also the parents of Ulfilas, who were of Cappadocian family but lived near Parnassus in a village called Sadagosthina . . . And he (Ulfilas) studied the ways (of the Goths) and having invented their special alphabet, he translated the whole of the Scriptures into their tongue." Similarly, in the Martyrdom of the great martyr Niketas (*Analecta Bollandiana*, Vol. XXXI, p. 211), it is stated that "Ulfilas, the bishop of the Goths, . . . invented the Gothic alphabet and having translated the Holy Scriptures into the language of the Goths, he prepared the way for the other barbarians to learn the Word of God."

[263] The Huns, the Houng-Nu of Chinese sources, being oppressed by other barbarians in Asia, made their way to the Volga and further west and began by subduing the Iranian people of the Alans, north of the Caucasus. Thereafter they harassed the Ostrogoths who at that time lay east of the Dniester. The Huns conducted their invasions on horseback, as savage nomads. To the peoples of Europe, who now saw for the first time representatives of the Mongoloid race, they presented a hideous aspect, which further contributed to the terror they inspired.

Constantinople, while Gratian came to his aid from the west. Before Gratian arrived, however, the senseless Valens rushed to attack the Goths who had already penetrated as far as Adrianople, near which city the clash took place. The Roman army was defeated, two generals were killed and Valens himself took flight and was subsequently burnt in a village where he lay hidden (388).[264]

Flavius Theodosius

After the defeat and lamentable death of Valens near Adrianople, Gratian summoned as co-ruler the Spanish general Theodosius, who in 378 had overcome the Sarmatians in Pannonia, and proclaimed him Augustus in Sirmium at the age of 33 (379 AD). Theodosius took up the administration of the East and was soon engaged upon the Gothic problem. The victorious Goths were making forays for plunder and aggressive raids; nevertheless Theodosius preferred to continue Gratian's attempts to reach an understanding. An understanding in fact ensued, by which Theodosius undertook to settle the Goths within the Empire and further, to supply them with provisions at need, while the Goths undertook military engagements towards the Empire as allies (foederati).[265]

The profitable terms of these agreements rendered the Goths arrogant; even so, Theodosius for a few years pursued the same conciliatory policy towards the Persians. From 387 to 390, instead of embarking upon a war with the Persians who were invading Armenia, he preferred to come to terms and to partition Armenia with them. The portion given to the Persians was thenceforward known as Persarmenia and comprised the greater part of the country. For this reason, Theodosius's agreement turned out to be of small advantage to Armenia, since it helped the Persians to establish a hold on that historic but unhappy country.

---

[264] See E. Stein. *Geschichte des spätrömischen Reiches*, Vol. I, p. 295 ff. For the Goths, see A. Vasiliev, *History of the Byzantine Empire*, 2nd. ed. (1964), p. 106 ff. I have been unable to consult in Athens J. Pierce's book, *The Reign of Theodosius I, History and Coinage*, 1938.

[265] See the "Life of Euthymius" by Cyril Scythopolites (Migne, *PG*, 114,600).

Religious Policy

Theodosius was much occupied with religious questions and wished to complete the work of Constantine. He fought paganism and Arianism and desired the unity of the orthodox Christian Church. After the death of its protector Valens the position of Arianism was insecure, since both Gratian and Theodosius were its adversaries. Only those Germanic peoples who had been taught Arianism by Ulfilas were destined to continue in it, and even these, in the course of time, became Orthodox Christians as they progressively became Latinized.

To ensure the realization of his religious programme Theodosius called the Second Ecumenical Council (381) at Constantinople, which was attended by 150 representatives from the East, but none from the West. This Council raised to the Patriarchal throne of Constantinople Gregory Nazianzene, [266] who, however, soon abdicated on account of objections to his election and retired to Cappadocia, where he died (390) after his long and faithful spiritual activity. The Second Council completed and confirmed the work of Nicaea in fixing the credal formulation of the orthodox conception of the Trinity. Besides this, in order to set bounds to the excessive ambitions of the Patriarch of Alexandria, the Second Council fixed the superior status of the Patriarch of Constantinople, second only to the Pope.

The great influence on the religious policy of Gratian and

---

[266] It is interesting to note what Gregory of Nyssa writes about the mania for theological discussion at this time: "Nowadays too, these same Athenians spend their time in nothing else but either to tell or to hear some new thing (*Acts* XVII, 21) starting up late and early from their workaday employments as amateur theological dogmatists. All sorts of house-slaves and jail-birds and runaway slaves philosophize solemnly to us about the ineffable mysteries. You cannot but have some idea of the kind of people referred to. The whole of the city is filled with people of this kind, the alleys, the market-places, the squares, the streets; there are hucksters in the clothing trade, money-changers, the men who sell us our victuals. If you ask for small change, the man philosophizes to you about the Begotten and the Unbegotten. If you ask the price of a loaf, the Father, it seems, is the greater and the Son subordinate. If you say you want a bath, the man lays down that the Son was created out of non-existence. I do not know what name we should give this plague, whether brain-fever or insanity or some such epidemic malady which causes a derangement of the mental faculties." (Migne. *PG*, Vol. XLVI, p. 557).

Theodosius was not Gregory Nazianzene but Ambrose, Bishop
of Milan, a famous orator and writer and above all a man of indomitable spirit and immense force of character. He was later
to humble Theodosius and even now, though absent, was
heard with respect; without himself being Pope, he was laying
the foundations of the Papal power.

In conformity with the religious programme which had
mainly been dictated by the fiery Ambrose, Gratian and Theodosius discarded the ancient title of Pontifex Maximus and
ceased in consequence to be religious heads of paganism as
well as of Christianity. They were therefore able all the more
easily to renew the struggle against the pagan cults. There
still remained, indeed, certain pagans who were respected by
Theodosius, men like Themistius, Libanius and, in the West,
Aurelius Symmachus who intervened in a number of questions
on behalf of the pagans. For the time being Theodosius overlooked this, but under the pressure of the relentless Ambrose
and Jerome (another Dalmatian) his anti-pagan policy grew
steadily stricter.[267]

One of the first measures taken by Theodosius was to abolish
the fiscal immunity of the pagan priests which Julian had decreed; but the most drastic step against paganism was the con-
fiscation of the endowments and gifts made to the ancient
temples, which, as we shall see, caused an outbreak of
revolt. In 391 it was decreed that apostasy from Christianity dis-
qualified a man from bearing witness in the courts of law and
it followed from this ordinance that Christians became the
only witnesses whose testimony was deemed reliable. In 393
Theodosius went further and forbade the ancient worship,
first in the East and later in the West.

It is understandable that this policy in religious affairs gave
rise to popular disturbances. In Egypt especially it seems that
Christian fanatics, moved also by hatred of the Greeks, among
whom many pagans were to be found. were the cause of massacres and other disasters. In Alexandria the bishop Theophilus
himself inspired the hostile movement and it was at this time
that the famous temple of Serapis, the Serapeum, was destroyed, the recently discovered Church of St. Menas being

267 J. Geffeken. *Der Ausgang des griechisch-römischen Heidentums*, 1920,
p. 154.

founded on its site. The pagans, however, did not readily give way to the Christians and there were many martyrs to their faith on both sides.

Pagan Insurrections

The policy of the hot-blooded Emperor from Spain provoked a concerted reaction on the part of the pagans, particularly in the West where they were more numerous. Theodosius, who had shown himself conciliatory towards the Goths and the Persians, was thus forced to enter on a struggle against two great rebellions by rivals whose chief support lay among the pagans.

The first of these rebels, Maximus, met with considerable success, since he captured and slew Gratian (383). Maximus was proclaimed Emperor despite the declaration against him addressed by Ambrose to the army. Theodosius was compelled to undertake a burdensome campaign in order to destroy his dangerous rival, which he did at Aquilei, near the modern Venice, in 388.

The second rebellion took place under the leadership of the former professor of rhetoric, Eugenius (392), who was himself a Christian but relied for support on the pagans in the hope that he would thus strengthen his cause and would be recognized as emperor. Once again Theodosius undertook a further expedition to the West, where in 394 he captured and slew Eugenius in northern Italy.

This was the last armed resistance of paganism, which had taken fresh heart from the era of Julian. Thereafter, in spite of the various persecutions, many pagans still survived until the age of Justinian, who removed their means of livelihood by economic attack, confiscations and other methods.

Oppressive Taxation

Theodosius proved a hard master, not only in his religious but also in his fiscal policy. He was in great need of money, on account of the settlement of the Goths, the rebellion, and the high cost of the imperial services. It was perhaps for this reason that he proceeded to confiscate the property of the ancient temples.

There were bitter complaints both from the taxpayers and from those who felt compassion for them. Besides the scourging and imprisonment to which the farmers were subjected, they even found themselves obliged to sell their children.

Thus, for example, the wife of one of them told the following tale: "On another occasion (the monk Paphnutius) found a beautiful woman wandering in the wilderness, having been driven out by the officers of the Governor and Council on account of a public debt owing by her husband, and as she bewailed her wandering life I enquired of her the reason for her lamentation. She replied: 'Ask me no questions, sir, and do not catechize me in my misery, but take me away as your servant wherever you will. For two years my husband was repeatedly scourged on account of a government debt of three hundred gold pieces, and was shut up in prison and my three darling children were sold, and I go my way as a fugitive, travelling from place to place. And now I wander about in the wilderness and often I am caught and continually flogged and for two days now I have remained in the wilderness without food.' And I (says the monk) took pity on her and took her away to my cave and gave her the three hundred gold pieces; and I brought her as far as the city, having freed her and her children and her husband." [268]

The following details regarding country folk and their fiscal oppression are reported by St. John Chrysostom but they are certainly valid for the time of Theodosius the Great: "Shall we then leave these examples and turn to other cases of men who to outward appearance are more respectable? And who are these? Those who have acquired landed property and reap their wealth from the earth. Yet what could well be more unjust than these men are? If one were to examine how they treat the poor, wretched farmers, one would find them more cruel than barbarians, for on those who are wasted with hunger and are overworked all their life long they lay continual and intolerable exactions and they load them with burdensome services as they might asses and mules and they treat them as if their bodies were made of stone, allowing them not

[268] *Palladius and Rufinus* (ed. Preuschen. XVI. 5, p. 72).

a moment's respite; and whether the land yields or does not yield, they rack them just the same and show them no mercy. What could be more pitiful than this, when after toiling for the whole winter and exhausting themselves with cold and rain and. lack of sleep, they return empty-handed and still deeper in debt, yet trembling and shuddering more at the thought of the bailiff's tortures and of being haled off to prison, and of requisitions and deportations and merciless impositions than at this hunger and rain?" [269]

These fiscal burdens caused a revolt at Antioch in 387 where in any case the indignation of the pagans was already great. In spite of the intercession of Libanius for his beloved fellow-countrymen, Theodosius showed harsh severity.

Ambrose

Theodosius proved still harsher to the people of Salonica. When in 390 the latter murdered the Gothic military commander of Illyricum, 7000 men were rounded up in the Hippodrome and killed. The impetuous Theodosius had indeed repented at giving the order for the massacre and had sent a second order cancelling the first, but too late.

The massacre at Salonica served to show how much power the Church could exercise through a fearless leader like Ambrose. When the news of the massacre reached the regional council of Milan, then in session, it immediately followed the lead of Ambrose who wrote to Theodosius that unless he repented and submitted to punishment he would cease to be a member of the Church. Theodosius thereupon did a thing which would have been impossible in the days of Constantine the Great. He submitted to the conditions and took Communion, after having knelt before Ambrose and sought the pardon of the Church.

The fanatical character of religious policy and the humiliation of the Emperor before Ambrose show that we are now in the Middle Ages. The age of religious toleration under Constantine and the early years of Julian's reign are long past. The world came to depend henceforth on the Church

269 Chrysostom. "Sermon 61 on St. Matthew," Migne *PG*, Vol. LVIII, p. 591.

and on religion, which could not leave the mind of man in freedom.

In 395 Theodosius died and left the empire to his two sons by his first wife, Arcadius and Honorius. Thereafter the Roman Empire was in fact divided, even though it still possessed the same laws and the same constitution.

CONCLUSION

In the two first chapters I have tried, although with a good deal of abbreviation, to show, even if only by a mere mention of the extremities reached, how the Greeks turned their backs on their homeland, the Balkan peninsula, and dispersed first to the coasts of the Mediterranean and the Black Sea, as far as the Lake of Maeotis (the Sea of Azov) and beyond the Pillars of Hercules as far as Tartessus, and later, under Alexander the Great, as far as India and Turkestan. Geographical, and subsequently economic, political and social reasons, and finally a romantic line of policy led to the incredible dispersion of Greek civilization and to its downfall, since the hundreds of thousands of Greeks in Magna Graecia, Syria, Egypt and elsewhere almost all became assimilated to the local inhabitants in the process of time and were lost to Hellenism. A Greek dispersion on a lesser scale took place in later times and further hundreds of thousands of Greeks were lost in Hungary, Roumania and Russia, and finally in America. It should be noted that in emigration it is the more vital elements of the population who leave and the biologically weaker elements who remain behind; it follows that, from this point of view, the emigration of so many hundreds of thousands of men to America and elsewhere in the space of one generation has been a fearful loss to modern Greece. If the ancient Greeks had firmly held on to the whole of the Balkans and Asia Minor, they would certainly have been the strongest nation on earth today and their influence would have been beyond calculation.

A special significance attaches to the Greek dispersion in Asia and Egypt where, after having rendered unique services to civilization in the third and second centuries BC, it gradually began, from 100 BC onwards, to sink into subjection to the religions of the East. The Greek dispersal, then, produced two great results: 1) the diminution and decline of the population of Hellas proper and its submission to the Romans, and 2)

171

the enslavement of the hundreds of thousands of Greek emigrants in Asia and Egypt to the various Eastern religions, as
was shown in Chapter VI above, though in a greatly abridged
account.

But the Greeks of Asia and Egypt, enthralled to alien religions, no longer resembled the ancient Greeks of Hellas
proper. They lost their lucidity of mind, they gave themselves
up to the obscurities of mysticism and were unable to give
guidance to the world. For when the Greeks were given over
to darkness and superstition, as the magical papyri and the
"Hermetic Books" of Egypt show us they were, who was
there to guide the world? The light of Rome was a borrowed
light, and when Greek civilization went into eclipse, Rome lost
her guide and she too "walked in darkness." She possessed
the blind discipline needed for the conquest of the world, but
in cases for which she had no Greek prescriptions to hand
she was at a loss what to do and led the world into a political
and economic impasse. We have said above that the Greeks
formulated the social problem but did not solve it in any
definitive fashion. Consequently, Rome had no prescription to
hand, such as she had for example in art or letters, and with
her military outlook, she attempted crudely, in the third century, to solve the problems of society and economics by the
aid of violence and the sword.

The Roman military government of the third century AD
was unable, in its simplicity, to grasp the fact that the world
had completely lost confidence in it and had taken refuge in
religion in the search for its salvation. The attempt of Rome
to stifle the Christian menace merely strengthened Christianity
further.

Constantine the Great did not invent but adopted and pursued the policy of religious toleration and a closer relation
with Christianity which had won the minds of the majority
of the population of the East, especially of the Greeks. This
retreat on the part of a personality as forceful, both politically
and militarily, as Constantine showed that a great turning-
point had now been reached in history, and that the Greco-
Roman civilization and the Greco-Roman world were becoming
mediaeval. This change signified the triumph of mysticism
and the fall of rationalism. The conquest of a variety of Eastern peoples by the Greeks, followed by the greater evil of

the Roman conquest with its consequent humiliation and exploitation of the subject peoples, caused rationalism to go bank-
rupt, so to speak, and fatally delivered mankind over to mystical religion. It is understandable that the appearance of Christianity with its proclamation of love and brotherhood should
perforce have overcome the other, lower religions of the
East, and it would have been strange if the temple-prostitutes
and slaves of the deities of Asia Minor, Syria and Egypt had
not gone over to the Christian religion in order to enjoy its
humanity.

The fourth century then, more especially from the time of
Constantine and owing to him, constitutes the most crucial
stage in world history. The results of the triumph of Christianity have endured to our own day and will endure much longer
still. But did the proclamation by Christianity of the doctrines of love, equality and brotherhood dominate and transform the human situation? Doubtless Christianity influenced
the noblest-minded men, brought into being great benefactors
to mankind and offered great examples of strict morality, but
it did not transform the whole of mankind. Even within
Christianity there were Christians who misinterpreted it,
hypocritical exploiters and tyrants, and those who tolerated
serfdom and slavery and the oppression of other Christians.
Besides the martyrs, heroes and saints of Christianity there
were also the theologians and the serfs, and the world was
to regard as its "Renaissance" the age which would set bounds
to the absolute dominance of mysticism and religion. Having
lost faith in mysticism too, the world was to turn its eyes
once more towards rationalism about the time that the Middle
Ages came to an end.

But let us not examine the whole significance of the Christian Middle Ages nor compare the advantages and short-
comings of mysticism as against the achievements and disasters of rationalism. We will only add a few words on the
significance of the fourth century in relation to the history of
the East Roman Empire.

The transference of the capital of the Roman Empire from
Rome to Constantinople contributed to the division of the
Empire into two halves, an eastern and a western, hastened
the final dissolution of the Western Empire by the Germans
(476 AD) and gradually delivered the Eastern Empire to the

Greeks. In the west the Germans had begun to establish themselves in the Roman Empire from the second century AD and by degrees they had overrun it, so that the liquidation of Roman rule by the Germans in 476 was not entirely surprising. But despite their vitality and despite their ability to create a state and a civilization of their own, the German invaders surrendered to the Latin tongue and became Romanized. Thus, those Germans who invaded France and gave that country its name from the Germanic people of the Franks learnt Low Latin and, with the ancient inhabitants, the Gauls, who had likewise become Latinized, they created a new language, French. The Latin language, therefore, helped to bring it about that the Germans who broke up the Roman empire quickly lost their German character and were assimilated to the older inhabitants of the so-called Latin countries (Italy, Spain, Gaul).

The great influence exercised by Latin was further helped by the Roman Church, which employed no other tongue and did not permit, so to speak, the creation of national literatures. The sole use of Latin strengthened the position of the Pope, who was able by degrees to establish and increase his power in spite of the overthrow of the western Roman Empire by the Germans. The example of Bishop Ambrose, who enforced the power of the Church against the Emperor Theodosius, and the doctrine proclaimed by St. Augustine in his famous work *De Civitate Dei*, that the Church, as the mandatory of God, is bound to direct the world, helped greatly to increase the Papal power and to make the Pope into a kind of ecclesiastical Emperor, who in spite of the decline of Rome and the creation of Germanic states wished to replace the secular power also.

In the East matters took another course. The State was from the first called Roman and it was Roman (it was given the name Byzantine in modern times), and as Christians, the eastern Greeks proudly called themselves "Romans" (Ρωμαῖοι), since they had to distinguish themselves from their heathen (ἐθνικοί) fellow-countrymen. The name "Greeks" ("Ελληνες) came to have a religious significance and was applied to non-Christians, even if these were Saracens. But if the name of Greek was laid aside and took on a special meaning, Greek culture was not laid aside with it. The transference of the capital of the Empire to Constantinople was by degrees to deliver its eastern half to the Greeks.

The Germans (the Lombards, the Gepids, but above all, the Goths) raided and harried the Byzantine Empire but they were few in number and were unable to exert any great influence on the development of the East. The Illyrians, and to a less extent the old native Thracians, who gave so many generals and emperors not only to Rome but to Constantinople (the houses of Constantine and Justinian, the general Belisarius and others) from the sixth and seventh centuries AD gave ground before the Hun and Slav settlements south of the Danube, lost their vigor and their worth and were gradually Slavized. As from the seventh century, the Byzantine Empire lost Africa and Syria, where there dwelt so many hundreds of thousands of non-Greeks (Syrians, Egyptions and others) who hated the Byzantine supremacy. From the time of Heraclius onwards the Byzantine Empire consisted of Asia Minor and the Balkan peninsula, less the northern provinces which became Slav. From the seventh century, then, the Byzantine Empire can be called Greek since the Armenians and those inhabitants of Asia Minor who were still unhellenized were gradually reduced in number. Those Armenians who attained the Byzantine throne by way of the army were already Hellenized.

But even before the Byzantine Empire had become practically uniform, that is to say Greek, from the racial point of view, it could not escape the influence of Greek letters. It did indeed employ the Latin language in its legislation until the time of Justinian, but with this exception almost all the rest of its intellectual life was conducted through Greek. The Church developed the whole of its literature in Greek, though without blocking the development of new literatures in other tongues such as Armenian, Coptic and Aramaic, as mentioned above. Christian men of learning, following the example of Basil the Great, Gregory Nazianzene and other fathers of the Church, read and profited by the ancient Greek authors, without being offended by their "heathenish" impiety. Some of them, like Photius, Aretas, and Eustathius of Thessalonike, studied, interpreted and copied ancient writers with a wonderful affection. Certainly, most of the Byzantine writers imitate the ancients and are under the influence of the ancient

Attic style, while from the fourth century AD onward the spoken language might be termed Modern Greek, since it had lost its ancient prosody and the distinction between long and short vowels and had acquired almost all its modern characteristics. It was only the impositions of Attic style and archaic imitation which hindered the use of the modern tongue.

The more or less complete imitation of ancient Greek, coupled with the dogmatic spirit imposed by Orthodoxy, hampered free creativeness; for this reason we cannot look to Byzantium for philosophic enquiries or for original work of the first order. The number of imitative poems, epigrams and other works was endless, but few of them can be read with gratitude or profit.

Yet, although we may condemn the excessive conservatism of Byzantium and its aping of antiquity, we must not forget that these antiquarians were concerned to rescue the works of the ancient Greek genius and to preserve them for the perpetual use of mankind. We must further remark that by its transmission of the Christian religion and by the translation of Christian and ancient Greek works into the Aramaic, Arabic, Armenian and Slavonic languages Byzantium also transmitted civilization to many peoples of Europe, Asia and Africa and rendered services comparable to those of ancient Greece. In particular, Arab science, medicine, philosophy, geography, mathematics and other branches of learning, were due in an incalcuable degree to the translations which Greeks or Hellenized Syrians made into Arabic. The loss of Syria and Egypt in the seventh century entailed a break of two centuries (from Heraclius to John the Grammarian and Photius) in "profane" literature, which had been particularly cultivated in those regions, but conveyed the wisdom of antiquity to the Arabs and stimulated the civilization known as Arabic.

But while the cultivation of letters at Byzantium was conditioned by ancient Greek, the other aspects of its internal constitution were governed by its geographical situation and its relations with its enemies. The Eastern Roman, or Byzantine, Empire from its very position sustained not only the constant succession of Persian attacks but also attacks by new enemies from Asia, who from the fourth century, from the Hunnish invasion of Europe, up till the fourteenth century and the attacks of the Ottoman Turks, delivered terrible blows against Byzantium. Above all, the Asiatic nations of the Bulgars, Arabs and Turks, both Seljuk and Ottoman, attacked Byzantium for centuries one after another, and the defense of Byzantium rendered supreme service to Europe, to which it afforded time to take shape and develop. The position of Europe would have been different, for instance, if in 717, in the time of the Isaurinan Emperors, the Arabs had taken Constantinople and had broken up the Byzantine Empire.

It must be noted that only a people with the economic strength of the Greeks could have possessed the financial means to enlist whole nations (the Alans, the Saracens, and others) in order to hurl them against the attackers from Asia.

But while the defense of Byzantium against the Asiatics was a service to European civilization, internally it gave rise to great upheavals and prevented an even economic and political development. The incessant defensive wars made it essential to produce competent commanders, from among whom the Emperors were necessarily drawn, and they naturally did not permit consideration to be given, for example, to the transformation of the monarchic constitution into a democratic one. But commanders who had fought gloriously in defense of Byzantium often became aggressive, and in consequence we often see that, besides the necessary wars of defense, Byzantium undertook senseless imperialistic wars of aggression, which worsened the internal situation. Military rule became arbitrary and caused frequent revolts; all too easily, it appropriated the possessions of the poor and gave rise to a social unrest which often found vent on the appearance of external enemies, Arabs or Turks, when the oppressed serfs or poorer classes ranged themselves with the adversaries of the Empire or did not serve it loyally against its enemies.

For this reason, we often find dissensions or rebellions, yet these never led to more radical political or social upheavals. The chief reason for this phenomenon, I think, is the outlet provided by the philanthropic activity of medieval Christianity, particularly Greek Christianity. From the time of Constantine the Great and Basil the Great, the Church and monasteries undertook, among their other duties, that of social welfare, and it may be said that the multitude of charitable foundations — hospitals, almshouses, orphanages and so forth — founded side by side with the churches and monasteries, sufficed to meet all the needs of the community and relieved the social distress which was caused by the injustices of military rule. Without a realization of this characteristic work of the Church we cannot properly understand the history of Byzantium or the number of the monasteries that were founded. It was the meeting of charitable needs which alone rendered the monasteries tolerable and indeed indispensible.

I have tried to point out a few essential features of the history of the Eastern Roman Empire which survived for more than a thousand years despite the unceasing attacks of Asiatic peoples, only because Constantine the Great transferred the capital of the Empire to the East and thus helped towards its gradual Hellenization. It was only because this Byzantine Empire was based upon the Greeks of Europe and Asia Minor that it was able to confer supreme benefits on European civilization and on a multitude of nations, services which are comparable with those of ancient Greece.

INDEX

Absolutism: foundations of
Roman, 128
Achaean Confederacy, 86
Achaemeodes, 125
Achilles: as "Lord of Pontius," 8;
as a god, 10; as a hero, 15, 35;
tomb of, at Illion, 153
Achilles, Tatius of Alexandria, 117
Acragas, 69
Actia: games at Nicopolis in
Epirus, 85
Actium: Battle of, 25, 85
Acts of the Apostles, 120
Administration: Roman, in East,
85-88; of Diocletian, 130; of East
under Theodosius, 164
Adonis: worship of, 96
Adrianople: 136; defeat of Licinius
by Constantine I at, 138;
penetration of Goths to, 164
Adrianou Therae, 115
Adriatic Sea: domination of, by
Agron, 26
Agean Sea, 2, 6, 8, 139
Aegina, Paul of, 112
Aelia Capitolina (Jerusalem), 82
Aelianus, Claudius, 114
Aelius, 17
Aemilius Paulus, 30, 71, 72, 73,
75, 80
Aeneas, Sophist of Gaza, 116
Aeolid of Asia Minor, 6, 41
Aeschines, 14
Aeschylus, 89
Aesculapius, 120
Aetius of Amida, 112
Afghanistan, 16, 52
Africa: 25, 43, 59, 62, 78, 106, 125,
149. 151, 175; inability of Greeks
to expand in, 13; reasons for
disappearance of Christianity
in, 77

Agape, of early Christianity, 103, 146
Agathe (Agde), 11
Agdistis, 92
Agelaus of Naupactus, 79
Agesilaus: father of Archidamus, 69
Agis, 40
Agriculture: inability to grow in
Greece, 5, 6; exchange of
Products of, 6; development of in
Egypt, 25,36; as help to trade.
37; new methods of, in Asia and
Egypt, 38; flourishing of in
Italy, 56; of Essenes, 97
Agrigentum in Sicily, 68
Agrippa, 72
Agron: Illyrian kingdom of, 26
Ahriman, 92
Ahura-Mazda (Ormuzd), 92
Aidesius, 153
Akragas (Agrigentum), 12, 70, 80
Alalia in Corsica, 11
Alamanni, 60, 130, 150, 154, 162
Alans, 177
Albanians, 1, 60, 80
Alexander: bishop of Alexanderia,
143
Alexander of Tralles, 112
Alexander Severus, 59
Alexander the Great: as leader of
expansion, 2, 3, 14, 171: dissolving
of Persian Empire by, 16; found-
ing of cities by, 17; successors of,
18, 19, 22, 24,, 36; final conquests
of 18, 28; example of, 26; render-
ing of service to mankind through,
28, 29; statue of, by Leucippus,
31; invasion of Asia Minor of, 34;
time of, 40; policy of, toward
religion, 91
Alexander the Molossian from
Epirus, 69
Alexander the Pope, 107